P9-ELG-655

What Is Postmodern Biblical Criticism?

A.K.M. ADAM

FORTRESS PRESS
Minneapolis

WHAT IS POSTMODERN BIBLICAL CRITICISM?

Excerpt on p. 69 from *Figure of Echo: A Mode of Allusion in Milton and After* by John Hollander. Copyright © 1981 The Regents of the University of California. Reprinted by permission of University of California Press.

Copyright © 1995 Augsburg Fortress. All rights reserved. Except for brief quotations in critical articles or reviews, no part of this book may be reproduced in any manner without prior written permission from the publisher. Write to: Permissions, Augsburg Fortress, 426 S. Fifth St., Box 1209, Minneapolis, MN 55440.

Scripture quotations from the Revised Standard Version of the Bible are copyright © 1946, 1952, 1971 by the Division of Christian Education of the National Council of the Churches of Christ in the USA and are used by permission.

Scripture quotations from the New Revised Standard Version of the Bible are copyright © 1989 by the Division of Christian Education of the National Council of Churches of Christ in the USA and are used by permission.

Library of Congress Cataloging-in-Publication Data

Adam, A. K. M. (Andrew Keith Malcolm), 1957–
   What is postmodern biblical criticism? / A. K. M. Adam
     p.   cm. — (Guides to biblical scholarship)
   Includes bibliographical references and index.
   ISBN 0-8006-2879-9 (alk. paper)
   1. Bible—Hermeneutics. 2. Postmodernism. 3. Decons-
   truction.
   I. Title. II. Series.
   BS476.A32 1995
   220.6'01—dc20   95-3485
                                                          CIP

The paper used in this publication meets the minimum requirements of American National Standard for Information Sciences—Permanence of Paper for Printed Library Materials, ANSI Z329.48-1984. ⊗™

Manufactured in the U.S.A.   AF 1-2879
99 98 97 96 95 1 2 3 4 5 6 7 8 9 10

For

Margaret Anne Bamforth Adam

ἑνί
πολυτίμῳ
μαργαρίτῃ

Contents

Editor's Foreword

The earlier volumes in this series for the most part participate in an unself-conscious way in the ethos of modernity. They share an orientation to the Enlightenment concern about sources, origins, and definitional and disciplinary precision. The present work, on the other hand, seeks to analyze the differences between the modern and the postmodern while self-consciously advocating a postmodern posture. It points out that postmodernism is not so much a method as a stance or posture composed of malleable and conflicting variables. The version of postmodernism presented here is characterized by three broad and encompassing features: Postmodernism is antifoundational in that it denies any privileged unassailable starting point for the establishment of truth; it is antitotalizing in that it is critical of theories that seek to explain the totality of reality; and it is demystifying in the effort to show that ideals are characteristically grounded in ideology or economic or political self-interest.

The Divinity School   —*Dan O. Via*
Duke University

Acknowledgments

This book would have arrived sooner—and probably been better—if a number of my friends and teachers had only gotten together to pool their wisdom and record the observations that appear on these pages. Since they missed their chance to join efforts and produce this book years ago, I have come along to relay what they would have told you, if only they had been here. The cast of characters on whose ideas I will draw includes Cornel West, Richard Hays, David Cunningham, L. Gregory Jones, Michael Cartwright, Stephen Fowl, Jonathan Wilson, and many more. Timothy Beal, Tod Linafelt, and Norah Shannon Planck subjected a penultimate draft to their critical gaze. The administrations of Eckerd College and Princeton Theological Seminary have provided encouragement and material support for my work, and I thank them heartily. I likewise thank the Publishing Director of Fortress Press, Marshall D. Johnson, and especially the general editor of this series, Dan O. Via, Jr.

Most of all I must thank two who have given me so much helpful advice that their own voices sometimes (helpfully) drown out my authoritative tones. Phil Kenneson patiently and diligently read the raw material of this work every week through the summer of 1993; he saved me from numerous egregious errors, and helped me at every step to realize what I'd been thinking when I said plainly foolish things. And Margaret Adam likewise scrutinized the whole manuscript as soon as I sent it to her, slashing my most long-winded sentences, checking my pedantry, and reminding me that this book is for readers (for whom she also prepared the index). These two generous souls permit the charade that this is a solo work, but you and I know differently. If there is anything erroneous remaining here, blame me; but if there is anything useful, anything illuminating, anything true, anything judicious, anything helpful here, think of them.

Preface

Before my readers wade any deeper into the hot springs of post-modern (poststructuralist?) theory and practice, they should be warned that virtually all the definitions and descriptions that follow are rejected by some insightful students of the phenomena I discuss. The risks are all the more considerable because the most careful versions of the theories I'll be describing can be intensely complex, and they have been painstakingly elaborated by subtle philosophers and critics. One cannot so much as broach these topics without taking sides in a slew of controversies, and in the following pages I will silently be taking sides at every turn. I will therefore try to avoid ascribing this point to Jacques Derrida, that to Jean-François Lyotard, and so on; this should help make the book an easier border crossing into postmodern theory. I will blithely oversimplify; I will summarize, report, and editorialize without specific advance notice. "Real experts" will want at each point to say, "It's a lot more complicated than that," or even "You're just plain wrong." They may often be right, but I have sacrificed nuanced exposition in the interest of introducing readers to postmodern reading practices without (I hope) intimidating or confusing them. I herein offer guidance not as a postmodern expert, but as an unauthorized transgressor; *caveat lector*.

That being said, I urge readers to plunge right in. Much of postmodern philosophy involves learning to think in ways we are not used to thinking; some readers may have difficulty figuring out what is going on, but most readers should eventually get used to these different ways of thinking and arguing by reading along. The real barrier to understanding and coming to terms with postmodern theory is not so much the complexities of the theories (although they can be complex) as their unfamiliarity. Students who are unfamiliar with the conventions of the historical-critical methods that are "normal" in academic interpretation often find historical criticism incomprehensible. Although some historical-critical tenets can be counterintuitive, the principal obstacle to assimilating historical-critical method is that beginning students are not accustomed to thinking in historical-critical ways. Both historical criticism and postmodern varieties of interpretation can seem quite intimidating on one's first encounter with them (I have known professors who took glee in shattering seminarians' "naïve" assumptions about the Gospels as well as avant-garde interpreters who enjoy shocking their audiences by propounding outrageous readings), but historical criticism and postmodern interpretive practices are much less unnerving once one has simply gotten used to them.

I expect that most readers of this small book will be much like the people I have known in various academies and congregations over the past fifteen years. At least, I will address readers that way, with a somewhat conspiratorial *we*. I will be delighted if readers who do not feel as if they belong among my assumed auditors would do me the honor of reading on, so that they may teach me things I ought to have known before I undertook this task.

Some specific advice: First, do not worry too much about what is really postmodern and what is not. Many critics think there are important distinctions to be made between postmodernism, poststructuralism, and various other epithets for a congeries of related interpretive phenomena. They are right, but we will muddle along without the benefit of their insight. This is not—at least, not exclusively—because I am congenitally wooly minded; I avoid this issue for several important reasons. One is that the hyperactive pursuit of precise definitions can itself be one of the marks of modernity; a postmodern introduction will be less likely to answer the question, "What is postmodern biblical criticism?" and more likely to answer the question, "What might postmodern biblical criticism be?" or, "What are some postmodern biblical criticisms?" Likewise, all the distinctions that critics suggest to lead us to the real, true, originary postmodernity exclude particular sorts of interpretation to which I feel obliged to introduce you. Finally, although at least one of the self-appointed purifiers of postmodern discourse is probably right, it is not at all clear who the right purifier is. So I suggest that you first taste the soup I prepare for you here; then, once you have learned more about the various ingredients, decide how you would refine the recipe.

Second, sometimes readers who are just getting acquainted with postmodern theory feel a certain disorientation. They feel that matters that are necessary to their understanding of rational thought, perhaps necessary to their self-understandings, are being rudely dismissed, without provision for some substitute that would help them get by. If you begin to feel as if postmodern theorists are telling you that everything you know is wrong, then remember that all the theorists whose arguments have influenced this book are more or less regular people—they stop at red lights, they pay their taxes, and they sign paychecks without a moment's hesitation. You, too, can continue your everyday life even if you accept the force of all the arguments here presented. You will probably think very differently about what you're doing, and you may well want to change some of the practices of your everyday life, but you will not have to go live in a tree and communicate by playing the flute.

Third, because these interpreters are regular people and they all disagree about important issues, you may be relatively confident that some of them are mistaken, at least some of the time. If you see compelling reasons to doubt their arguments, you are in good company. At the same time, you would do best not to dismiss their claims hastily, but to assay them for the truths to which they might point. Even critics who believe that postmodernism is gravely misguided recognize that these multifarious movements have taught philosophy, theology, and biblical interpretation some important lessons.

Fourth, you will encounter the word *discourse* repeatedly throughout this book. It is a convenient word that postmodern theorists use to point toward the ways our theoretical discussions of particular topics do not float about in splendid isolation from "real life," economic motivations, political decisions, and so on. A discourse thus includes the intellectual theories and arguments on a given topic, but also the ways such a discussion is entangled in the everyday conditions of people's lives. The discourse of biblical interpretation, for example, involves not only important books on hermeneutics, but also the academic systems by which universities and seminaries determine who may teach biblical studies, the publishing industries that determine what one may read, and the denominational hierarchies that determine who may preach (to specify but a few of one discourse's ingredients). In a postmodern context, the word *discourse* should help remind us of the complex interaction among the theoretical and practical components of our various interests.

Finally, if Jeffrey Stout's delightful "Lexicon of Postmodern Philosophy" (*Religious Studies Review* 13 [1987]; reprinted in a different version as an appendix to his book *Ethics after Babel* [Boston: Beacon Press, 1988]) is easily available, read it as an entertaining warm-up to the adventures before us. If Stout is not handy, then think for a while about Michel Foucault's dictum, "To work is to try to think something different from what one thought before," or about the neon sign that has hung in front of the Lenbachhaus Gallery in Munich, which bears a similar message:

YOU CAN THINK THE OPPOSITE

1
Textures of Postmodernism

Postmodern thought is not one thing. Indeed, most postmodern thinkers would argue that it cannot and should not be just one thing; most varieties of postmodernism strike out against the very notions of identity and unity in one way or another. As a result, there are as many varieties of postmodernism as there are people who want to talk about the subject. One satirical article points out that everything from fashionable hats to ski parkas to pastries to situation comedies claims to be "postmodern" (*Spy*, April 1988). Some varieties of postmodernism are quite at odds with others; some varieties can coexist fairly calmly, and indeed some are quite harmonious with one another; and still others (the ski parkas) are quite vacuous. If, in the course of your explorations, you find one certified post-modern thinker making claims that another postmodern thinker polemi-cizes against, you ought not be surprised; just chalk it up to the enduring capacity of the topic "postmodernity" to start heated arguments under any circumstances.

Even if postmodernity is not any one thing, it is some things more than others. It is almost always fair to think of postmodernism as a movement of resistance. The name itself suggests that postmodernity defines itself over against "modernity." Postmodern thinkers have typically discerned a pattern of radical problems with the ways many of us have gotten accus-tomed to thinking and arguing; they want to resist the bad habits we have fallen into under the influence of modernity.

We are often unaware that we have intellectual habits that someone might question. One of the principal characteristics of modern thinking is the notion that humanity has progressed to the highest pinnacle of achievement under the aegis of Enlightenment Euro-American efforts. Moderns typically assume that every day, in most ways, the world is getting better and better. This attitude stands in sharp contrast to the view (which was once commonplace) that matters were better long ago in a Golden Age, and that they have gone downhill since then. At about the Renaissance, some people started thinking in a different way; they reckoned that people might have gotten better, rather than worse, since the dawn of time. These new thinkers contrasted the way people had thought in the past with their own way of thinking (which they called *modern*, from the Latin word *modo*, "currently"). This intellectual conflict was called "the Battle of the Books" in England, and *la Querelle des Anciens et des Modernes* ("the debate of the Ancients and Moderns") in France. The Ancients argued that the classical artists and authors had known the qualities of beauty, truth, and grace better than any contemporary artist could. The Moderns argued that knowledge of these matters was progressive, and that contemporary writers and artists could know more than their classical predecessors, because they had the benefit of the classical writers' counsel and the added experience of a millennium of deliberation on aesthetics. The Moderns made fun of the ancients for idolizing classical authors. They pointed out that even Homer was subject to grave errors in literary judgment: Odysseus's dog, for instance, would have had to be at least twenty years old to recognize his returning master, which was an unbelievably old age for a dog. Jonathan Swift, who enlisted on the side of the Moderns, satirically deplored the Ancients' reverence for Homer:

> We freely acknowledge Him to be the Inventor of the *Compass*, of *Gun-powder*, and the *Circulation of the Blood*: But, I challenge any of his Admirers to shew me in all his Writings, a compleat Account of the *Spleen*; Does he not also leave us wholly to seek in the Art of *Political Wagering*? What can be more defective and unsatisfactory than his long Dissertation upon *Tea*? ("A Digression in the Modern Kind," *A Tale of a Tub, with Other Early Works, 1696–1707*, ed. Herbert Davis [Oxford: Basil Blackwell, 1965], p. 80)

The Moderns argued that the simple condition of having lived and worked long ago was itself a problem for the Ancients and that living and working in the modern world puts us significantly ahead of our forebears.

One conclusion that the moderns drew from this was that there is an ever-growing gap separating the past from the present. This was not always the way people thought about their relation to the past. If we think of the medieval paintings that show Abraham dressed in armor and Melchisedek dressed as a bishop, or if we read about David and his "knights" in the fifteenth-century *Speculum Humanæ Salvationis*, we realize that people used to think of the past and the present as joined in close continuity. They did not imagine that life had been significantly different even fifteen hundred years before. But contemporary biblical interpreters reflect a different, more specifically modern outlook when they work vigorously to distinguish themselves from the interpreters who have gone before them; only the most recent scholarship carries compelling rhetorical weight in biblical studies, and the more recent, the better. Articles in the *Journal of Biblical Literature* or *Interpretation* are likely to cite sources only from the last twenty years or so. Like the first moderns, modern biblical scholars set themselves over against their past, and defend the newness of their own conclusions.

Another characteristic of the transition to modernity follows from the initial rebellion against the ancients. Before the moderns, one could resolve arguments by appealing to the authority of the ancient sources. But if the moderns had progressed beyond the ancients, modernity obviously required a different criterion for distinguishing legitimate from illegitimate arguments. Whereas the ancients had legitimated their conclusions by appealing to the content of what they claimed (that is, "Does this agree with what the great minds of the past taught us?"), the moderns adopted a criterion based on the method by which one reached the conclusion in question: reason. Modern thought looks to the rationalism of the European Enlightenment as its epitome. Modern thinkers adopt Immanuel Kant's motto, "Dare to think!" and insist on the radical freedom of their inquiries. So long as the study is rational (or more precisely, we may use the German word *wissenschaftlich*, "scientific" or "scholarly"), it is justified; if the conclusions are properly reasoned, they are true. Thus modernity ascribes tremendous authority to scientific study and considers any deviation from rational inquiry unthinkable. When biblical interpreters insist on rational, scientific explanations of biblical events, or when they defy traditional interpretations in the name of free scholarly inquiry, they show a debt to modernity.

One of the consequences of the modern pursuit of formal scientific truth is that scholars divided the terrain of possible inquiries into several formally separate spheres. They decided that the scientific search for the truth of art is distinct from the scientific search for the truth about nature, and both differ from the search for the truth about ethical behavior. Each of the spheres of intellectual endeavor has its own self-defined, self-contained kind of rationality (natural science, ethics, and art are the three spheres endorsed by Hegel and Kant, but other thinkers would slice the intellectual pie differently; more recent thinkers tend to cut the pie into more slices). And anyone who would participate in the scientific search for truth in a particular sphere must learn the particular sort of rationality that determines the truth of that particular discipline. This aspect of modernity comes to the fore when biblical scholars distinguish their work sharply from, for example, theological reasoning; modern biblical interpreters insist that these two forms of inquiry must be kept scrupulously separate.

When we divide inquiry into autonomous (self-regulating) spheres, however, we soon reach a state where no one person can master the specific rationalities required of each sphere. Instead, one must specialize in one sphere or another in order to attain the degree of fluency in the discipline that permits one to count as a practitioner of that particular science. In other words, modern knowledge is specialized knowledge, which is fully accessible only to credentialled experts. One can see the characteristics of this outlook when, in the recent controversy over the Dead Sea Scrolls, some scholars alleged that the scrolls should be kept secret lest they engender a spate of "bad scholarship"; in typically modern fashion, the translation committee feared that allowing nonspecialists access to the scroll fragments would only contaminate knowledge of the scrolls' contents. In similar ways, the institutionally approved faculty members in various academic disciplines constituted their fields as more or less *wissenschaftlich* fields of inquiry, gradually regulating access to the privilege of speaking authoritatively on disciplinary matters.

These are characteristics of the current academic intellectual world; even as some scholars submit that this is the postmodern era, most intellectuals and academies continue to function comfortably along typically modern lines. Modern biblical scholars typically distance themselves from earlier interpreters, many of whom were immersed in allegorical and typological approaches to interpretation. At the same time, modern scholars emphasize the extent to which the Bible is time conditioned, a product of past ages to which we no longer have access. They proclaim a gap not only between the former biblical interpreters and us, but just as much between the Bible itself and us; we can't simply read our Bibles and understand what we see, because of the gap that divides past and present. That gap can be bridged, according to these moderns, only by *wissenschaftlich*, scientific inquiry. In the field of biblical scholarship, that means interpretation with a rigorous historical focus which excludes any trace of theological determination. Luckily for us, the modern academy

4

produces suitably trained biblical historians to whom we can turn for legitimate modern interpretations of the Bible.

This overview of modernity and its impact on biblical interpretation may seem rather pointless. It may seem that I have simply related to you what common sense already dictates: that appropriately educated experts have privileged authority to interpret texts whose historical setting is so remote from us as to be virtually unintelligible, and that these experts should conduct their inquiries without biases from their particular theological standpoints. The point in rehearsing this capsule of background on modernity is to point out that the assumptions we modern biblical interpreters make are not eternal truths, but are habits that we have gotten into after an earlier long period in which we had different habits. The impetus toward a postmodern approach to philosophy, to art and literature, to life in general—including biblical interpretation—comes when critics begin to see some of these habits as unnecessary, and others as downright bad.

A STARTING POINT

What are the biblical interpreters' (putatively) bad habits? Everyone has a different list (of course). Cornel West, who works in the fields of philosophy and theology, has suggested in lectures at Yale that we approach postmodernism as "antifoundational, antitotalizing, and demystifying." Postmodernism is antifoundational in that it resolutely refuses to posit any one premise as *the* privileged and unassailable starting point for establishing claims to truth. It is antitotalizing because postmodern discourse suspects that any theory that claims to account for everything is suppressing counterexamples, or is applying warped criteria so that it can include recalcitrant cases. Postmodernism is also demystifying: it attends to claims that certain assumptions are "natural" and tries to show that these are in fact ideological projections. All these characteristics deal with one of the most common characteristics of postmodern thinking: postmodern critics characteristically problematize *legitimation*, the means by which claims about truth or justice or reality are validated or rejected. These characteristics—antifoundational, antitotalizing, demystifying—are not exhaustive, but they provide a useful beginning point for exploring postmodernity.

One of the pivotal moments of modernity came when René Descartes realized that he could not doubt his own existence; from this, he rebuilt the whole metaphysical superstructure of Western philosophy with this one axiom as his foundation. Descartes's *"Cogito, ergo sum"* ("I think, therefore I am") provides a cogent example of philosophical foundation-alism: There is at least one certain truth on which we can rely, which we can use to support all our contingent speculations. One need not adopt the *cogito* as one's foundation, of course; one may cite the unvarying character of human nature, or God's indubitable revelation, or the progressive self-revelation of *Geist* ("Spirit, Mind") through time. Whatever one's foundation, the philosophical tradition has customarily assumed that one needed to have some undoubtable, unshakeable truth with which to back up one's theoretical claims.

Postmodern thought undermines this assumption of an unshakeable truth in a number of ways. Most simply, postmodern theorists point out that no foundational belief has successfully commanded general assent; what good is a foundation for bolstering one's theories if one's opponents doubt the foundation itself? The postmodern critique runs deeper than this, however, for it may not be possible for foundations to exist at all. If there is such a thing as a strong foundation, it must be immune to any but capricious or perverse objections; yet in order to judge a claim "un-doubtable," we need to know beforehand what kinds of claim we should doubt and what kinds we shouldn't. And if our would-be foundationalist philosopher obliges us by trotting out a distinction between dubitable and indubitable foundations, the postmodern critic can point out that this distinction is evidently more fundamental than was the proposed foundation. Moreover, the critic can demand to know what criteria enable the foundationalist to know dubitable from indubitable foundations—and if the foundationalist is so patient as to answer this challenge, the postmodern critic can simply repeat the same challenge and the same question infinitely. Philosophical foundations are never foundational enough.

Foundations do not secure philosophical discourse because discourse itself is a human construction, and humans have certain characteristics that complicate the project of putting together a foundation. In the first place, a "foundation" would have to provide an account of perception that both allowed for such phenomena as optical illusions or false memories, and at the same time explained how one could distinguish the real, true, perceived reality from the supposedly unreal, false reality, which an optical illusion represents. Obviously a foundation that one cannot distinguish from an illusion is useless; the precise importance of a foundation is that one cannot doubt it. If, however, we assemble our foundation from data that we collect with faculties whose workings we must always question, how sturdy can the foundation be?

Moreover, even if we could identify a foundational truth that was not subject to problems related to perception, we would not be able state it clearly enough for it to do a foundation's work. Humans communicate their philosophical foundations with words and symbols; but words and symbols are in every case ambiguous. Anyone who has dealt with hormonally supercharged adolescent boys knows that they can turn any remark into a sexual innuendo. The capacity to discover unintended multiple meanings is not a peculiarity of adolescent males (although the aforementioned topic may be), but is a general condition of human communication. Our capacity to communicate about what is or is not foundational is defined by our capacity to communicate about anything. And because philosophical foundations are supposed to make our conclusions obviously unquestionable, an ambiguous foundation is as bad as no foundation at all. Indeed, an ambiguous foundation is even worse than none, for at least when one has no foundation, one does not suffer from a false sense of security. The problem is not that our perceptions or our communications deviate from some putative standard of "reality"—that would simply reinscribe us in a modern effort to define reality more and more precisely—but that the inherent ambiguity of human perception and communication renders them unfit elements for anything so rigid as a foundation. It is, to adapt a biblical metaphor, like building one's foundation of sand.

Postmodern philosophers argue that foundations simply are not necessary. They do not do the work one asks of them, and they simply provide one more point to which an opponent can object (as opponents surely will). Just as people got used to the idea that the earth is not immovably fixed at the center of the universe, so they can get used to the idea that our arguments, claims, convictions, truths, rules, and so on do not depend on having an absolute philosophical (or theological) foundation. The world and meaning may be in flux, but some things fluctuate more slowly than others; if we think and argue carefully, the absence of a foundation won't trip us up.

Postmodern thought dispenses with totalities as well as foundations (in fact, a "totality" needs a foundation to hold it up). Modern customs typically stress the necessity of theories or rules that universally apply. A theory must apply to all members of a given set, under all circumstances (or at least, under circumstances that are exhaustively controlled). The universality in question may be cosmic: the contemporary search for a Grand Unified Theory or Theory of Everything in physics reflects the modern quest for a total physical theory. Modern theories of interpretation frequently depend on the notion that there is something about being human that underlies claims about valid interpretation. This hypothetical common human essence would enable all human beings to respond sympathetically to certain themes or images. If we want to understand a text from a distant culture, we can—on a modern account—enter into the text's world on the basis of the humanity we share with the text's original authors and addressees.

"Totalities" do not have to be universal sets of certain kinds of things (or of everything), however. A totality may be restricted to a particular unitary set. Modern thought has established the pivotal importance of a rather smaller totality: the individual, who subsists as a self-contained totality of experiences, thoughts, feelings, desires, and so on. The individual is the centerpiece of modern thought; the one thing Descartes could not doubt was his own existence. Modern thinking distinguishes sharply between what is proper to the individual (what you have seen with your own eyes, your own belongings, your skills) and what is imparted or imposed from circumstances beyond the individual. The "nature vs. nurture" controversies about child rearing reflect this habit; theorists search diligently to determine just which characteristics belong to the individual as her own nature, and which are the result of forces from beyond the individual.

Postmodern thinkers generally resist such totalities. Totalities, after all, either include everything altogether or proceed by excluding some possible members. If the totality includes everything, it is intellectually useless; after all, what is there to say about "everything," and who are we to say it? The sort of totality that serves some useful purpose works by differentiating members from nonmembers, human from nonhuman, individual self from not-self. But the process of exclusion requires us to make judgments about what is in and what is out. This is where problems with totalities come in: Who decides what counts and what doesn't? Remember the problems we touched on above when we were worrying about foundations; many of the same problems apply when we make judgments concerning totalities. To return to the example of the alleged "human essence," if someone who looks more or less human reads *King Lear* without being moved by the king's folly and suffering, do we decide that she is not human after all? Or that *Lear* does not really appeal to something universal in humanity? If we want to argue that a common human essence underlies the world's most magnificent literary achievements, we will have to admit either that people who do not appreciate such literature are not fully human, or that no works attain the level of true greatness. If on the other hand we stipulate that works need the approval only of some human beings, we need then to explain what justifies promoting those particular people to their position of authority. We will likewise have to account for all the apparent human beings who are grievously out of touch with the common human essence that we posit. (We will have to explain, for example, why the vast preponderance of works that defenders of humanity nominate for universal significance have been composed by men in Europe and North America; are Euro-American males especially in touch with what is universally human?)

There is moreover a fairly simple argument against our claiming a human totality. Just whom would we trust to decide who is human, who is not? We have seen thus far that other humans have a relatively poor track record for ascertaining what counts as humanity; at various points, the United States government has considered women, African Americans, and Native Americans to be insufficiently human. In certain circumstances, gravely ill people are judged not to have rights that presumably pertain to all human beings. When can we be confident that we have really understood what it means to be human? If we cannot be sure that we have attained that degree of wisdom, then what business have we claiming that one or another trait is essential to our being fully human?

Totalities are problematic at the individual level as well. The very fact that there are long-standing controversies over the extent to which individuals are determined by their innate qualities as opposed to the qualities evoked by their environment suggests that the very distinction between what is innate and what is external may be blurry.

Michel Foucault provides one famous example of a postmodern critic interrogating the notion of totalities. Foucault wonders just what should be included in "the complete works of [Friedrich] Nietzsche": "We will, of course, include everything that Nietzsche himself published, along with drafts of his works, his plans for aphorisms, his marginal notations and corrections. But what if, in a notebook filled with aphorisms, we find a reference, a reminder of an appointment, an address, or a laundry bill, should this be included in his works?" (*Language, Counter-Memory, and Practice*, p. 118f.). Foucault's question is especially pertinent for Nietzsche, inasmuch as Nietzsche left many unpublished manuscripts. (It is relevant for Foucault as well, because there is now a small controversy over whether the numerous interviews Foucault gave should be counted as equal to his other "works," or as subordinate to the finished books and essays.) Among Nietzsche's unpublished fragments was the isolated sentence, "I have forgotten my umbrella," which diligent French editors have compiled into their edition of his *Die fröhliche Wissenschaft* (*The Joyful Wisdom*) (fragment #12,175, cited in Derrida, *Spurs*, n. 18, p. 159).

Enter Jacques Derrida, who points out that the editors' decision to include the umbrella into their version of this specific work is fraught with complications. This gesture obviously raises again the question of what an author's "complete works" are, but it also then poses a challenge to the notion of authorship. After all, Nietzsche never authorized the publication of an edition of *Die fröhliche Wissenschaft* that included the forgotten umbrella; the umbrella's place in Nietzsche's works depends on subsequent editors' decisions. Even if the phrase is excluded in future editions, the resulting work will be the product not of Friedrich Nietzsche alone, but will reflect a collaboration between Nietzsche and later editors. The "Nietzsche" whose name appears on the title page of future editions of *Die fröhliche Wissenschaft* will necessarily include the editorial judgments of Nietzsche's literary heirs: the name "Nietzsche," which designates the "unified" author of the "total body of" work, will have expanded to include the editors.

It can be just as difficult to formulate a clear notion of "the individual" as it is to explain what an author's complete works are. We have a hard time specifying just what we mean by "the individual" or "the self." If we are talking about a mental or psychic entity, are we then separating "the self" from the body? If the self includes the body, is the self diminished when the appendix or some part of the body is removed? Our customary use of terms like "self" and "individual" covers up the extent to which those words do not refer to any one thing, but to a fluid collection of impressions, thoughts, feelings, and physical entities. There is no single, self-present entity that one might specify is "herself" or "himself." Our everyday language nods to this difficulty when we say of a friend who is surprisingly impolite one morning, "She's not herself today"; we mean something like, "She is behaving in ways that do not reflect her usual character." In either case, our idiomatic observation recognizes that none of us is just one persona; we are the intersection of a numerous personas, any one of which may manifest itself at a given time.

In short, postmodern critics observe that none of these totalities—the universe, humanity, the self, or any other—can ever do the work that modern discourses give them to do. Perhaps the totality in question has excluded embarrassing counterexamples, as when one ascribes universal human significance to *King Lear* and overlooks the numerous people to whom *Lear* is uninteresting and irrelevant. Or perhaps "unity" has been

10

imposed by rhetorical force on a heterogeneous congeries of facts, arti-
facts, and impressions, such as an author's "complete works" or a person's
"identity." Totalities are always in flux; but a totality in flux simply isn't
total enough.

Of course, we no more need totalities than we need foundations. If we
specify the domains of our claims more carefully, we can make arguments
that have local—rather than (hypothetically) universal—relevance. In
most cases, an appeal to what is supposedly universal serves most often
as a stick with which to beat recalcitrant opponents. Something "universal" would be unquestionable, and anyone who resisted "universal" truths
would thereby be exposed as a nihilist, an anarchist, someone with a dan-
gerously perverted mind. But postmodern critics can avoid totalizing
claims without shredding the social fabric. Indeed, to the extent that postmodern interpreters exercise humility about whether we can know "universal" truths, or ascertain the limits of a "unity," or plumb the depths of
an "individual," they avoid the presumptuous tyranny that claims that "we
know the truth about you" on the basis of some "universal" theory of what
makes a person human. Postmodern critics attend to the particularities of
specific cases more than to the generalities of universal categories.

These universal categories of which modern thought is so fond frequently serve as self-authenticating warrants for theoretical or ethical arguments. The modern critic claims that his point can be derived from the
very nature of reason, or that human nature obliges us to think in certain
ways. Postmodern opponents will typically latch onto such claims and—
using language derived from Marxist economic analysis—suggest that
these appeals to abstract universal entities are mystifications of more con-
crete, worldly reasons. That is, the postmodern debater accuses her modern partner of concealing mundane (economic, political) motives behind
a screen of universality or necessity. This is the demystifying tendency
that Cornel West suggests is characteristic of postmodernism.

One could easily make the case, however, that demystifying has played
a leading role in specifically modern thinking. The rationalist criticism of
theological doctrine, the Marxist critique of capitalism, the psychoanalytic
critique of consciousness, all partake in the demystification of institutions
and functions which had been thought "natural" or divinely ordained. Demystifying, in fact, provides one of the most familiar gestures in modern
discourse: the dramatic sweep with which the critic unveils the grubby
interests and motives that drive even the most high-minded and (apparently) disinterested institutions. When an analyst dismisses religious faith
as wish fulfillment, when a political agitator points out the extent to which

11

the electoral process is restricted by financial considerations, they display the characteristically modern "hermeneutics of suspicion," which looks in every closet to discover the lurid secrets that are surely concealed there.

Nevertheless, modern inquiry has generally restricted the scope of this demystifying suspicion to particular classes of institution and theory. Certain domains have remained above suspicion precisely because they wield the flashlights and microscopes for searching closets. The postmodern tendency toward demystifying addresses the demystifiers themselves: science, reason, and liberal democracy (to name three leading subjects of postmodern interrogation). In demystifying the assumptions of these institutions, critics are not undertaking a distinctively postmodern practice, but are directing a modern practice against itself (and therein lies the postmodernity of postmodern demystifying).

Modern science, for example, was very suddenly engaged in a bitter struggle with theology over which of these disciplines provided a more truthful account of the the place of earth in the solar system, over the origins of human life, the age of the earth, and so on. Scientists won this conflict—they provided arguments and evidence that eventually persuaded the preponderance of the participants in the dispute that the disciplined pursuit of scientific conclusions was a reliable source for truth. If one doubts the extent to which science established its domination of the field of truth telling, one ought to consider not only how many studies in the "humanities" (history, literary interpretation, art criticism, and even the production of art) have sought to bolster their arguments by appealing to "scientific" warrants, but also how few studies in the sciences have tried to enhance their rhetorical clout by claiming to be more "humanistic" or less scientific. Even the defenders of literal interpretations of the biblical accounts of creation and miracles, who are often thought the most tenacious forces of resistance to modern science, often ground their arguments not primarily on the trustworthiness of the Mosaic or apostolic testimony, but on "creation science." The natural sciences set the agenda and defined the rules for truth telling in Western culture.

Several decades ago, however, some historians of science started to question the degree to which science stood up to its own criteria. A freight load of works questioned the extent to which scientific disciplines could claim privileged access to representing the truth about the world. One oversimplified account of this process would take as its point of departure the recognition that one cannot separate scientific "facts" from the theories and experiments that produced them. Instead, one must look at the

12

production of scientific truth somewhat as one looks at the production of automobiles: if one sets up an assembly line for pickup trucks, it will not produce convertible sports coupes, no matter how many units the line produces. In order to produce a sports coupe, one must introduce the possibility of producing sports coupes into the assembly line itself. To return to the field of science, an experiment will only produce a fact for which the experiment has been prepared; if the preparations have been inadequate, or the designer of the experiment has made a serious mistake, then the experiment will produce few significant results or none, just as a poorly planned assembly line will produce poorly built trucks, or few trucks, or pickups with no room for carrying anything. When a failed experiment allegedly produces the discovery of a new scientific fact, we will usually find that the experimenter imaginatively reconfigured the original experiment in order to account for the initial failure, that she then formulated an alternative account of her experiment to explain why the first experiment seemed to fail, and that she then tested her new alternative in an experiment designed to produce particular results. The initial experiment did not suggest the new discovery; the scientist reconstructed her interpretation of the available data, then constructed a new experiment that produced the data she expected.

If scientists only find data that fall within the range of what their experience and imagination permit them to find, then the discourse of science is inescapably built on theories—not on hard data or observable facts. The theories that scientists use to imagine experiments, to make it possible to interpret what happens in an experiment, to deem some aspects of an experiment important and others unimportant, all combine to constrain the results a scientist obtains. Moreover, all scientific experimentation depends at crucial points on our perception, but we observed above that perception is simply not a suitable foundation on which to build. Science has no compelling basis for claiming a privilege in determining the truth about the way things are.

The problems with science run even deeper than the limits of experience and imagination, however. Think about the biggest problems currently facing science: all involve research that requires equipment of a very specialized and powerful kind. Such equipment does not come inexpensively; only very well funded investigators can afford to conduct scientific research. The funds available to subsidize such research are usually attached to very durable strings; the amount of funding one can generate is typically proportional to the usefulness of one's research for military or industrial purposes. Even research that fits neither military nor industrial needs must produce results of some kind; scientists cannot simply fiddle around in their laboratories, waiting for an interesting occurrence, but must produce a steady stream of (publishable) research results. Scientific research is thus persistently overshadowed by questions of profit; a scholar who is not producing publishable or profitable research results will be in constant jeopardy of losing her funding, and scientists whose research is profitable will be expected to keep the useful research results coming. In neither case is science the pure, disinterested search for truth on which its ideological function as a privileged arbiter of truth claims depends. Instead, scientists weigh the political consequences of various research programs, all of which involve particular vested interests in particular ways. Science is locked in a delicate power struggle for its identity, balancing the importance of "pure research" against the exigencies of financial support for experimental research.

The same points apply all the more in other discourses of demystification. Reason, the cardinal virtue of modern philosophy, does not exist in an atemporal transcendental zone. Instead, the attributes of "rational" discourse change with time, and with the problems that one is discussing, and with countless other variables. Whereas the advocates of reason have typically upheld the importance of rational deliberation by setting reason over against tradition, we find that the very nature of reason is always dependent on the ways particular traditions have interpreted "reason"! A demystifier who argues that belief in a resurrection is "irrational" is, in effect, claiming no more than "that's not the way people like me reason." There are many people like this hypothetical rationalist, and they represent a powerful tradition, but (as Alasdair MacIntyre has shown in a series of works) they are nonetheless arguing on behalf of one tradition against another tradition. And the second, "proresurrection" tradition has included some of the most committed advocates of reason in the history of the West.

When modern rationalist demystifiers appeal to "reason," without specifying what sort of reason they mean, they are mystifying their own debt to one particular tradition of reasoned inquiry. They cover the particularity of their intellectual position by treating reason as if it were a natural universal category. Postmodern demystifiers will turn the tables on the modern critics and posit that this appeal to a naturalized, universalized conception of reason is nothing other than a power play. It short-circuits argument: If we agree to regard reason as universal, then the argument is over and the moderns have won; if we do not recognize reason as universal, then the moderns regard us as irrationalists, and the argument is over, and we are no longer on speaking terms with the moderns.

In both these cases, the moderns have typically presupposed that the specific attributes of their intellectual tradition—a reliance on science and scientific method, and the transcendental authority of reason—were immune from the sort of demystifying that they applied to every other pattern of thought. Postmodern thinkers, however, have applied the demystification with which science and reason examined the world to science and reason themselves. Their investigations suggest that science and reason are inevitably constituted by the intellectual traditions in which they stand, are implicated in (personal and) political struggles, and are inevitably subject to "subjective" biases in countless ways. In fact, we may confidently suppose that whenever people sit down to establish a single theoretical system that would have a privileged relation to the Truth, they will contaminate the purity of their theory with decisions we can attribute to personal interests, unscientific interests, unresolved psychological determinations, or any of dozens of impure, nonuniversal motivations.

So Cornel West's three characteristics of postmodern thought turn out to be intimately related to one another. Postmodern criticism cannot accept any system of knowledge as absolute or foundational; it cannot accept the premise that some body of knowledge, or subject of knowledge, constitutes a unified totality; and it cannot accept mystifying claims that any intellectual discourse is disinterested or pure. Where the moderns dreamed of establishing an absolute, unified system of all purely rational knowledge (symbolized, for example, by the idea of the encyclopedia), postmodern critics will ceaselessly stress the extent to which these dreams are illusionary (and sometimes quite nightmarish). Postmodern thinkers will not look for an absolute foundation, but for a starting point suitable for their purposes (this is one reason articles of postmodern criticism so often begin with short accounts of apparently insignificant or irrelevant incidents). They will not try to explain everything about the world, or an author, or a specific work, but will sketch a series of interesting relations among certain aspects of one or more topics. They will not claim privileged access to the truth, but will simply claim to have provided a provocative reading of the topics they engage. Where modern criticism is absolute, postmodern criticism is relative; where modern knowledge is universal, unified, and total, postmodern knowledge is local and particular; where modern knowledge rests on a mystified account of intellectual discourse, postmodern knowledge acknowledges that various forces that are ostensibly external to intellectual discourse nonetheless impinge on

15

the entire process of perceiving, thinking, and of reaching and communicating one's conclusions. Nothing is pure; nothing is absolute; nothing is total, unified, or individual.

FURTHER POSTMODERNITIES

While Cornel West is one particularly helpful annalist of postmodernity, he is certainly not the only, or even the most important, scholar to discuss the qualities and implications of postmodern theory. Jean-François Lyotard (whose essay on *The Postmodern Condition* is probably the most widely cited source on the subject), Fredric Jameson, and numerous other critics have argued for various further characteristics of postmodern thinking. Most of these are correlates of the characteristics we have just examined.

The most prominent of these further claims is Lyotard's observation that, "Simplifying to the extreme, I define *postmodern* as incredulity toward metanarratives" (*The Postmodern Condition,* p. xxiv). "Metanarratives" (or "grand narratives") are the stories we tell about the nature and destiny of humanity: Hegel viewed all history as the gradual self-revelation of Spirit (*Geist*) through time, while some people talk about the progressive recognition of innate human rights and of emancipatory evolution toward liberal democracy, while others talk about the inevitable rise and fall of capitalism that will prepare for the workers' paradise, and so on. Lyotard suggests that modern thought has relied on metanarratives like these to supply the warrants for its own distinctive agenda; if we can assume that the world is really evolving toward universal recognition of human rights and political democracy, then our efforts to speed up and enforce that evolution are justified. If the existing institutions are the necessary products and support system of this metanarrative, then they need not be questioned, nor ought they be attacked. Lyotard argues that metanarratives like these can no longer sustain the importance with which they are loaded—and the general cynicism of contemporary political and economic life tends to confirm Lyotard's position.

This "incredulity toward metanarratives" fits our initial sketch of postmodernity well. What, after all, are metanarratives good for? First, they provide a narrative foundation for our way of life: we go to war in the interests of the (unquestioned) universal value of liberal democracy, or we relish the proliferation of soda pop drinks because more choices means more freedom for the consumer. Then, too, metanarratives function to define and enforce totalities. The very name of the now defunct

16

congressional House Un-American Activities Committee illustrates this principle; once we know what constitutes the American Way, then we know who is an American, and who is not, and we know that the metanarrative of American supremacy justifies our punishing citizens for being "un-American." Finally, the metanarrative conceals the extent to which our practices and assumptions have meanings quite apart from their context in the metanarrative. We may explain a United States military assault on a small, non-Euro-American nation with reference to America's defense of liberty and human rights. If we say no more, however, we hide the facts that there were other ways to nurture greater freedom in the country in question, that the United States does not indiscriminately invade countries ruled by tyrants, but does so selectively, and that the decision to invade was made in a specific political context by officials who had a stake in appearing decisive and powerful.

Modern metanarratives serve as intellectual expedients that plaster over cracks in the projects of modernity. If one questions the universal authority of scientific truth, a modern interlocutor may demand, "Would you want to try to survive without contemporary medicine, without electronics, or even electricity?" The postmodern point is not that medicine and electricity are bad; the point is that we judge them good from within a way of life that already depends upon them, and are therefore in no position to decide whether they are desirable for people who do not already depend on these modern appurtenances. Moderns, however, will see contemporary science and technology as valuable in themselves, such that all societies should be introduced to the blessings that have made contemporary Western life what it is. Moderns will tend to interpret deviation from their particular party or political lines not only as disloyalty, but as irrationalism or anarchism. This is especially true with regard to deeply engrained elements of the metanarrative; someone who suggests that "human rights" or "freedom of choice" are not the highest good for people is immediately suspected of fascism or Nazism. Postmodern critics of metanarratives will become wary when metanarratives intrude into argument. Is the metanarrative functioning to explain why a speaker thinks the way she does, or is the metanarrative supposed to close off the argument by positing a last-word legitimation of one side's position?

A critic who stresses metanarrative incredulity as the definitive mark of postmodernism may want to chastise the (Christian) Bible's pretension to tell the story of everything from Creation to Apocalypse; there are sources galore for metanarratives here, as the history of interpretation has well illustrated. Yet one may well observe that there is no single clear metanarrative of the Bible (in its Christian forms, even less so in the Hebrew Bible). The various components of the Bible interweave and argue among themselves. A careful reader is as likely to come from the Bible amazed at its internal contestation as she is to see its tyrannical, monotonous unanimity.

This points to another mark of postmodern approaches to textual studies. While modern critics have tended to emphasize the reader's direct engagement with the text and the autonomy of the text itself, postmodern critics are inclined to recognize much more complexity in the interaction of text and reader. The text, after all, has certain physical characteristics, which already generate certain expectations; if one sees a leather-bound book with ribbons marking various places therein, one does not usually expect to find that the book in question is a gothic romance or an accounting textbook. This is not because there is an intrinsic opposition between novels or accounting texts and leather bindings with ribbons. It is because our culture reserves such expensive and imposing luxuries for books of particular sorts of significance. Cultural mediation, however, does not stop with the book's appearance. The reader herself will have been predisposed to regard the text in specific ways; a reader who grew up outside synagogue or church life, who is attending a state university, is more likely to see the Bible as a din of conflicting theological claims than is a reader who grew up with frequent participation in worship, who is attending a Bible college.

Some critics have adopted an emphasis on the reader's experience as the hallmark of a postmodern approach to interpretation. These critics argue that their orientation toward the reader's experience of meaning rather than toward a meaning presumably encased in the text marks them as truly postmodern. It profits us little to quibble over such points, but one should approach such claims cautiously. If reader-response critics persistently discuss the text's formal characteristics and how the reader is compelled to react to textual stimuli, if these critics pay little or no attention to the social and institutional location that defines their experience as readers, then their emphasis on "the reader" may reflect a modern predilection for self-identical individuals reading autonomous texts. More unnervingly postmodern readers will observe that this modern reader-response picture is far too simple.

After all, one's interpretations depend on one's commitments to various social institutions, on the interpretations of one's closest peers and colleagues, and on the experiences to which one has been exposed in life. The postmodern critic would point out that countless mediations complicate the modern picture of a single reader encountering an autonomous text. A more postmodern picture would show dozens of colleagues looking over the reader's shoulder, with employers and various other institutional officials alternately dangling money and picking the reader's pocket. The text would not be an autonomous object of contemplation, but would be shown with representatives of sundry interpretive interests, some of whom are highlighting particular passages, others obliterating passages, others adding words here and there, and still others thrusting filters between the reader and the text.

The forces complicating our analysis of reading a text are both social and institutional. Stanley Fish has emphasized the extent to which our relations with other people shape our readings by describing what he calls "interpretive communities"; I would argue, however, that Tony Bennett's term, "reading formations," is more useful. Whereas "interpretive communities" (especially as Fish describes them) sound like clubs that are defined by particular hermeneutical rules, I find that "reading formations" reminds me of the various conflicting economic and social constraints that compete for the reader's allegiance. Both terms, however, undermine the possibility of using the reader-text interaction as a reliable foundation for objective interpretations. Likewise, these postmodern perspectives break down the putative totalities of "text" and "reader"; here, a crowd of readers (of whom "the reader" is at best only the committee chair) encounters several different versions of "the text," which shimmer and shift, chameleon-like, into further different texts.

Of course, the readers of the Bible have long been aware of the problem of figuring out what *the* text of the Bible is. The Hebrew canon? The Septuagint with the New Testament? In which English translation? And what about such textual problems as the ending of Mark's Gospel, or the story of the woman found in adultery? But such difficulties are not confined to ancient texts; there is a current bitter argument over the correct text for James Joyce's twentieth-century novel *Ulysses* as well (and don't forget Nietzsche's umbrella, as Nietsche himself evidently did). These are the most obvious examples of a text's instability, but a postmodern critic can calmly make the case that no two people ever read the same text twice. There is no "*the* text."

If in postmodern accounts there is neither a unified, totalized reader, nor a unified, autonomous text, then no more is there an "author"; postmodern interpretations are, in a word, "unauthorized." Even more than various modern reading formations have privileged "the text" or "the reader" as the locus of interpretive power, they have stressed the unshakeable privilege of the author as a constraint on interpretation. The meaning that the author intended in composing a text is the single most widely held criterion by which modern interpretations have been judged legitimate or illegitimate. The author, who is usually long since dead, exercises an unearthly power of compulsion over interpreters, who are obliged to seek out one golden fleece of interpretation: the author's intended meaning, which is, paradoxically, always inaccessible. Roland Barthes has gone so far as to pronounce "the author" dead—not just particular authors, but the whole notion of authorship. This comes as no surprise, of course, to attentive readers of the preceding pages, who remember the difficulties that Derrida and Foucault pointed out with regard to the notion of Nietzsche's complete works. For postmodern readers, "the author" is a fragmented, contested range of possible identities; the modern unified, unambiguous author who authorizes only particular, correct interpretations, no longer exists.

Because "the author" is never a unified, unambiguous totality, "the author" is just as unsuitable a foundation for criticism as "the text" or "the reader." Postmodern interpreters need not feel any more bound to authorial intentions than to autonomous texts or unified readers. After all, the interpreter's role is always to speak for the author, to say *in loco auctoris,* "This is what I really meant." We do not have access to "the author's intention," but always only to the interpreter's notion of what the author intended—a notion that may or may not be right, but that is always provisional, debatable, and certainly not the same as the original intention itself. Postmodern interpreters may operate freely without fear of ghostly authors looking over their shoulders, coercing them to obey "original intentions."

Indeed, as postmodern criticism escapes modernity's fascination with time, the many assumptions modern people make about "originality," "progress," and "time-conditioning" are more problematic. For example, the modern biblical interpreter assumes that there is a great gap between past and present, which he must valiantly bridge using the tools of historical analysis. The postmodern interpreter, however, may point out that there is already a substantial bridge, inasmuch as the Bible has been interpreted continuously for the whole time that the modern critic is concerned with. The expositions of these intermediary interpreters offer testimonies to the text's meaning, which are invalid only on the modern assumption that one has to reckon with the chronological gap. If, with a postmodern interpreter, we decline to make the chronological assump-

20

tion, then our need to reckon with the gap disappears, and we can once again learn about the text from our premodern colleagues. The assumption that interpretive inquiries must have their foundations in a text's original context in the past does not necessarily hold for postmodern readers; the past (especially as historians reconstruct it) is not a unified whole into which a text fits. Instead, the postmodern past is a cacophony of conflicting stories whose narrators shout to be heard. There is no *"the* past" to be found. Once again, as with "author's intentions," so with "the past": when a modern interpreter insists that the historical record of the past makes his interpretation of a text the best, he is always only talking about *his own interpretation* of that historical record. "The past" changes every time a historian mounts a successful rhetorical campaign to persuade people of one or another account of the past; modern interpreters who claim otherwise mystify the connection between the past they claim to be really true with the past reconstructed in their own work.

Likewise, if we exorcise the demon that obliges us to think of the past as distant and inaccessible, and of the present as newer and better, then we can begin to recover from our modern addiction to novelty. So long as modern assumptions govern interpretation, we will participate in an endless leapfrog game, wherein each scholar must continually generate "new knowledge" (whether that knowledge is valuable or trivial, it must at least be new; that is the principle on which doctoral programs thrive). The hunger for novelty and up-to-dateness drives the proliferation of books and journals, but one may fairly wonder whether that unquenchable desire benefits anyone else. Postmodern critics are often careful to avoid arguing that their perspective has finally overcome modernity, for that would simply reinscribe postmodernity into the modern cycle of overcoming and being overcome. Modernity will not be vanquished, it will not be done away with, but postmodern critics can invite their audiences to consider whether modern or postmodern ways of reading are more fitting for their lives. Italian philosopher Gianni Vattimo applies the German words *überwinden* ("conquer, overcome") and *verwinden* ("recuperate from, get used to" and in some cases, "twist, distort") to these two ways of addressing modernity. If we try a conquest (*Überwindung*) of modernity, then modernity will always win; the notion of progress, which sees ideas in conflict and assumes that the stronger idea defeats the weaker, is fundamentally modern, so that if modernity's antagonists try to eliminate it, they become that which they have tried to destroy. If, on the other hand, postmoderns simply get used to the persistence of modernity,

21

their resignation (*Verwindung*) opens an opportunity for them to live and think in nonmodern ways within the continuing cultural dominion of modernity.

Finally—for now, at least—postmodern criticism is willfully transgressive; it defies the boundaries that restrict modern discourses to carefully delimited regions of knowledge. I noted above that biblical interpreters and theologians usually draw a sharp distinction between their two domains; even so, the two seem to be more closely allied than, say, biblical interpretation and landscape architecture. The postmodern interpreter, however, gleefully ignores the boundaries that dictate what one may say at which academic convention, or in which sort of criticism. Where modernity demands expertise of anyone who speaks of a given discourse, postmodernity observes that a large part of the process of becoming an expert involves learning certain things that one may not say. Postmodern transgressors will not respect the shadow of any disciplinary Father who would hold them accountable to the laws of that particular field of knowledge or communication. Postmodern critics—to appropriate Jonathan Culler's metaphor (*In Pursuit of Signs*, p. 118)—rub texts together to see what sparks will fly, what will perhaps catch fire. Or they may playfully blur the distinction that separates history from fiction, or literature from criticism, or interpretation from politics. The postmodern reader recognizes that the rules of interpretation are provisional guides rather than commandments carved in clay tablets; they are not foundations, or natural laws, but the habits and styles that our teachers have passed down to us in the craft of criticism.

So, to summarize, we recognized earlier that postmodernity can be antifoundational, antitotalizing, and demystifying; in these last pages we have found that postmodernity may also be incredulous toward metanarratives, oriented toward reading formations rather than readers and texts, unauthorized, indifferent to time and time conditioning, and transgressive. Of course, a particular postmodern essay need not be all of the above at once; many postmodern theorists stress only one or two of these characteristics, and some argue that only one or two are truly postmodern. The family relations among these traits provides ample reason to treat them all here, however. When the interpreter makes one or another of the moves described above, we have grounds for discerning the influence of the postmodern.

These characteristics of postmodern criticism do not—*pace* numerous worried modern scholars—lead to a chaos of absolute relativism. First of all, we must point out that there is no more possibility of an "absolute" relativism than of an absolute foundation, or an unambiguous totality, or a natural obligation; even relativism is impure. There are always constraints on interpretation; or, more to the point, there are always constraints on what one may expect other people to accept. After all, there never will be binding constraints on what interpretations one may expound, for there always will be interpreters whom we regard as eccentric, or deluded, or insane, who will insist that the Apocalypse of John refers exclusively to them. They will not be deterred by new, improved hermeneutical theories. At most, we can hope to devise a theory that clarifies why some interpretations seem more persuasive than others, and how we can learn to generate and adopt these more convincing interpretations.

But if postmodern scholars have made their case persuasively, we are no worse off for our lack of absolute foundations, or unified totalities and individuals, or pure discourses. Postmodern critics do not doubt the existence of starting points or totalities so much as they doubt that these are ever unproblematic. If you recognize that, you will be a good way toward getting comfortable with postmodern thought. While a modern scholar assumes that history is the absolute horizon for biblical interpretation, a postmodern explores what interpretation would be like without an absolute horizon. This is part of the reason postmodern thought exasperates modern people so—it makes thinking difficult by questioning the habits to which we have grown accustomed. At the same time, this is what makes postmodern thought so important; not all habits are good, nor are all shortcuts safe (and the character of "goodness" and "safety" are themselves always slipping, always open to revision). Perhaps this is the most important lesson of postmodern thinking: We cannot guarantee either the correctness or the soundness of our thinking by adopting the right method, or by starting from the right point. Or, for that matter, by not starting at all.

Further Reading

There is no end of articles and books on postmodernism. Curious readers will be best served by acquainting themselves with the writings of the prominent postmodern theorists themselves, although the opacity of some such texts can be intimidating. One might begin with Jean-François Lyotard's explanatory book, *The Postmodern Explained*, trans. and ed. Julian Pefanis and Morgan Thomas (Minneapolis: Univ. of Minnesota Press, 1993), which clarifies and expands upon his earlier book, *The Postmodern Condition*, trans. Geoff Bennington and Brian Massumi, Theory and History of Literature, vol. 10 (Minneapolis: Univ. of Minnesota Press, 1984), which itself includes a useful foreword by Fredric Jameson. (Jameson develops his own analyses of postmodernism in *Postmodernism, or, The Cultural Logic of Late Capitalism* [Durham, N.C.: Duke Univ. Press, 1991].) Geoff Bennington has surveyed Lyotard's wide-ranging career in *Lyotard: Writing the Event* (New York: Columbia Univ. Press, 1988). Cornel West advocates a postmodernism grounded in the American tradition of pragmatic philosophy in "The Politics of American Neo-Pragmatism," in *Post-Analytic Philosophy*, ed. John Rajchman and Cornel West (New York: Columbia Univ. Press, 1985), and *The American Evasion of Philosophy* (Madison: Univ. of Wisconsin Press, 1989). Jürgen Habermas resists postmodernism in the name of a better, more conscientious modernity in essays such as "Modernity versus Postmodernity" (*New German Critique* 22 [1981]: 3–14) and in his *The Philosophical Discourse of Modernity*, trans. Frederick Lawrence (Cambridge: MIT Press, 1987). Alasdair MacIntyre's work on reason and tradition appears in the very difficult *Whose Justice? Which Rationality?* (Notre Dame: Univ. of Notre Dame Press, 1988) and in his *Three Rival Versions of Moral Enquiry*, Gifford Lectures for 1988 (Notre Dame: Univ. of Notre Dame Press, 1990). Stanley Fish's work on "interpretive communities" appears in his very readable *Is There a Text in This Class?* (Cambridge: Harvard Univ. Press, 1980); he develops his approach to the problems of theory and meaning further in *Doing What Comes Naturally* (Durham, N.C.: Duke Univ. Press, 1989). Tony Bennett's article "Texts in History: The Determinations of Readings and Their Texts," from *Post-Structuralism and the Question of History*, ed. Derek Attridge, Geoff Bennington and Robert Young (Cambridge: Cambridge Univ. Press, 1987), 63–81, introduces his use of the term "reading formations." Michel Foucault's essay, which mentions Nietzsche and his umbrella, is "What Is an Author?" in *Language, Counter-Memory and Practice*, ed. Donald F. Bouchard, trans. Donald F. Bouchard and Sherry Simon (Ithaca, N.Y.: Cornell Univ. Press, 1977); Derrida's reflections on this point appear in *Spurs/Éperons*, trans. Barbara Harlow (Chicago: Univ. of Chicago Press, 1978), 122–43, cf. nn. 14, 20. Among other important theorists, one should consult Julia Kristeva, whose work one may sample in *The Kristeva Reader*, ed. Toril Moi (Ithaca, N.Y.: Cornell Univ. Press, 1986), and Gianni Vattimo, who argues for a postmodern attitude of *Verwindung* ("resignation" or "twisting") to modernity in *The End of Modernity*, trans. Jon R. Snyder (Baltimore: Johns Hopkins Univ. Press, 1988). Jonathan Culler discusses some of these issues in *The Pursuit of Signs* (Ithaca, N.Y.: Cornell Univ. Press,

1981). Steven Best and Douglas Kellner provide an overview of many of the issues and theorists in *Postmodern Theory* (New York: The Guilford Press, 1991).

Robert Fowler specializes in reader-response criticism, which he sees as a postmodern interpretive maneuver; look over his *Let the Reader Understand* (Minneapolis: Fortress Press, 1992) and "Postmodern Biblical Criticism" (*Forum* 5/3 [1989]: 3–30) if you are curious about his approach. Edgar McKnight's *Postmodern Use of the Bible* (Nashville: Abingdon Press, 1988) is quite lucid; the first half is especially useful for its emphasis on textual indeterminacy, but the second half propounds the more questionable conclusion that postmodern readers of the Bible ought to adopt a reader-response, literary-formalist approach. Walter Brueggeman's *Texts under Negotiation* (Minneapolis: Fortress Press, 1993) is a another helpful guide to postmodernity and its relevance to biblical studies. Stephen Moore's *Literary Criticism and the Gospels* (New Haven: Yale Univ. Press, 1989) is both extremely helpful and extremely well written; it does not deal so much with postmodernism in a broad sense, but is an unsurpassed survey of its domain in New Testament studies. For still further reading, consult the notes and bibliographies of the above-mentioned works.

2
Deconstruction: On Making a Difference

Deconstruction is . . .

One could not begin a chapter on deconstruction less felicitously than by using the words "Deconstruction is . . ." The problem is not just that many people think that deconstruction (not deconstruction*ism*, please) is many different things. As we saw, many people believe postmodern thought to be many different things, yet we ventured numerous characterizations of postmodernism. The problem is that one of deconstruction's principal goals is to alert us to the dangers of that most familiar and ostensibly innocuous word *is*. Let us begin, then, not by saying what deconstruction is, but by saying that deconstruction works to show that any interpretation, any sort of communication or even thinking, entails serious risks, which we customarily avoid recognizing. Deconstruction *does* more than it *is*. (Timothy Beal suggests to me, "Deconstruction happens.")

We will begin with the most difficult bit. Such a beginning is poor rhetorical strategy, but we will venture it in the hope that readers will get past these intensely daunting paragraphs before they even notice, and that they will then enjoy sledding down the smoother slopes of subsequent sections. One recurring strand in the cable of deconstructive argument is the problem of "presence," that is, the presumption that there are things to which our words refer, to which our thoughts correspond, with which we interact unproblematically. Deconstructive thinking regards the presumption of presence as a foundation (in the sense we used last chapter) of all the dominant Western cultural systems. In order to learn from deconstruction, we need to suspend our assumption that our words refer to things, that our expressions mean things, that there are, in fact, "things" at all—including ourselves.

In the language that deconstruction appropriates from structural linguistics, deconstruction questions the supposed connection between the "signifier" (the word, or gesture, or image, or symbol, or sound) and the "signified" (the meaning of the word/gesture/image/symbol/sound). Deconstruction involves showing that there is no necessary connection between signifier and signified. Even such proper nouns as "Robert Dole" do not entail a direct, unambiguous connection between signifier and signified; there are surely several citizens named Robert Dole, and even if we were to assume by fiat that there were only one (or that only one of them made a difference), the name is not the politician. The proper name fills in for the person whom it signifies. It is the person's representative, but not the person; not even proper nouns escape the tangles of signification. Another useful illustration of this principle is the way various languages use different words to signify the same object. There is nothing about a maple that makes it inherently more fitting to call it "a tree" or "un arbre" than "a taxi" or "a paramedic." We use one rather than another because of an elaborate set of conventions that regulate our use of language.

In this respect, deconstruction sets out to resist what Derrida has called "logocentrism": a commitment to the principle that there is finally some metaphysical thread connecting words and their referents, signifiers and signifieds, and that if we can only find the right approach (or method, or foundation, or origin, or first principle), we can discern the *logos* of the cosmos. Unfortunately, this logos is always subject to the question we posed to foundations in general—how do we know that this is the foundation? How do we know that this is the logos? One cannot answer such a question without grounding the foundation in some warrant that is then more foundational; the warrant one provides then becomes a deeper, more solid, new foundation. But when one chooses not to justify one's chosen foundation—"It's just true, and that's that"—one's proposed foundation looks suspiciously arbitrary. Neither justifying nor refusing to justify is suitable for so grand a phenomenon as a philosophical foundation. If one justifies adopting it, it is no longer the foundation, but if one declines to justify adopting it, it is quite arbitrary. By posing the how-do-we-know question, deconstruction displaces the logos from its position of authority; deconstruction decenters that which has been constructed to be central.

There! Now, that was perhaps startling, but not so very unintelligible. It follows relatively smoothly from the antifoundationalism of the first chapter. If there can be no foundations to our lives, then surely there can be no inviolable relations between words and things, nor can there be necessarily any "things" at all. If there were, we would have some foundation on which to ground our philosophical system.

Deconstruction gets at this difficult part by way of the insight that nothing exists of itself; anything about which we say, "Yes, that is a thing" exists by virtue of our distinguishing it from other things. In the domain of interpretation, we distinguish a *u* from an *n* by noting whether the round bit is at the top or bottom of the letter; this distinction, in our idiom, "makes a difference." The idiom points to precisely what deconstructors want us to notice, however: differences are not natural or given, but are made. The government has no interest whatever in the proportion of blue-eyed to brown-eyed employees of a given company, but it is intensely interested in the proportions of men and women, and of various racial groups (but only certain groups; some racial groups make a difference, and others do not). Identity (the archfoundation of all our philosophical and theological foundations) is constructed when people decide that certain distinctions make a difference, and others do not. There is thus no natural, or innate, or simple "sameness," or "is"-ness.

The simplest way to construct identity involves drawing an absolute and simple distinction (what structuralists call a "binary opposition"): male/female, animate/inanimate, white/black, truth/falsehood, original/copy, center/margin, objectivity/subjectivity. Deconstructive thinkers note that these pairs always tend to favor one of the members; the first member tends to be defined as normal or normative, and the second member as not-the-first, or less-than-the-first. Recall for a moment the biblical warrant for designating the female human being: "She shall be called woman (*'iššah*) because she was made from man (*'îš*)." This way of making a distinction inevitably relegates the "other" term to derivative, secondary importance, and it typically makes an explicit value distinction between the terms. Man is primary, woman secondary; light is good, darkness evil, and so on. At the same time, the first term cannot subsist by itself; it depends parasitically on the excluded second term. When we construct binary oppositions that favor one term over the other, we build the arbitrary preference for the first term into the structures of our linguistic practices. Moreover, because no thing escapes being enfolded into the flux of language, we build the arbitrary preferences into the world.

Once again: If identity is always only constituted by way of difference, then there can be no absolute identity anywhere. All identity is necessarily relative to things-it-is-not. Therefore one cannot define what a term or a thing or a persona or feeling *is;* there is no identity there to specify, but only differences from other things. There are no *things* there; only not-the-other-things. In a deconstructive nutshell, there is no presence that escapes being entangled in the infinitely vast tangle of differential relations. There is no center by which we can orient ourselves with respect to the margins, nor is there a real essential identity (or unity) that we can then distinguish from its various characteristics. Paradoxically, we are not even identical to ourselves. Our supposed identities are a composite of countless different identities: Kathy as a daughter, Kathy as an acquaintance, Kathy as a student, Kathy as a parishioner, and so on. If we endeavor to strip away all these incomplete identities, we do not arrive at the one, true essence of Kathy. Apart from all the partial identities, we discover no identity at all (or, to put it positively, we only ever know Kathy as one of these partial identities). The illusion of a unified self is a projection of our overwhelming desire for presence.

Some of these claims probably appear paradoxical and antitheological. If there is no personal identity, if there is no center, if there is no presence that transcends the flux of difference, if deconstruction wants to displace the Logos at the heart of logocentrism, then there hardly seems room for notions like "God" and "the Word." Similar objections would apply to deconstruction's relation to philosophy and literature as well; how and why does anyone continue to talk about "things" and "texts" if these are as undecideable as deconstructors say? Why should we care what deconstructors argue when we (winking with an affected Parisian flair) know that the authors of deconstructive criticism don't really exist, and that their supposed texts are simply effects of the differential flux? Such questions as these lie at the heart of the protests—some enraged, others simply pained, still others honestly baffled—against the epidemic of French letters that seems to be invading academic discourse.

These dilemmas involve crucially important aspects of deconstruction, and they are well worth considering. In order to come to grips with them, we need to recognize that deconstruction does not abandon verbal communication, or the general discourses of philosophy or literature (or theology). Likewise, deconstructive arguments are not exempt from the deconstructive critique they level at others. Instead of withdrawing into autism, deconstructive readers continue to take part in their discourses "in a certain way" (a phrase Derrida uses in several of his important essays when he addresses just this problem). Deconstruction does not, after all, teach us that communication or knowledge or transcendence is impossible; it teaches us that these matters are awkwardly entangled in the various discourses. The entangling becomes especially awkward when the

30

participants in a particular discourse claim that a certain topic is foundational or central to their discourse, at the same time that they acknowledge that this central point always escapes being enclosed by the discourse. For example, historians claim to be telling the real truth about history (How did William of Orange annex Ireland? What were relations between the American colonists and Native Americans really like?), but the controversies and changes that shadow their work constantly testify to the extent to which "the real stuff" of history eludes their grasp. (What would a history be like if—to suppose the impossible—it told the whole truth about even a single incident? It would be like a map with a scale of 1 inch : 1 inch—perfectly accurate, and perfectly useless.) Deconstructive criticism strives to take this constant elusiveness seriously while continuing to work along with the various discourses.

Deconstructive critics can operate in various ways. The most familiar deconstructive maneuver is probably a hyperbolically close reading of a text; this painstakingly minute deconstructive examination reveals ways in which the text always undoes the arguments it is ostensibly making. The deconstructor in caricature pulls on a loose thread in the fancy garment, then chortles gleefully when the whole garment unravels and falls to pieces. (In fact, when deconstructors do this sort of work—and I will undertake a little, toward the end of the chapter—the point is usually not to poke fun at hapless textual victims, but rather to point out how complicated is the enterprise of figuring out what is going on with respect to the text in question.) Deconstructive critics can develop various other strategies for inhabiting their chosen discourses. They can continue playing by the rules of a given discourse, but persistently point out how those rules cross one another, cancel each other out, and obstruct the presumed goals of the operation. They can continue to play by most of the rules of a given discourse, but diverge from those rules at particular points, in particular ways (thus forcing other participants in the discourse either to ignore the deconstructor's intervention, or to devise some way of accounting for this new mode of participation), or they can blur the boundaries that separate discourses, or ignore the boundaries altogether.

When deconstruction moves into the discourse of biblical criticism, it displaces many of the cardinal characteristics of institutionally legitimated interpretation. First, it underlines the antifoundationalism that we have already described; there can be no absolute reference point by which we orient our interpretations: not the text, the author, the meaning, the real, historical event, nor any other self-identical authoritative presence. Second, it implies that when an author tries to compose a text that overcomes the limitations we have been discussing, she will inevitably fail; there will always be traces of the exclusions and the distinctions that do not make a difference, which a careful reader can locate and use to undermine the rhetorical power of the supposedly authoritative text. To allude once again to chapter 1, deconstruction demystifies the putatively unquestionable oppositions (say, for example, that which separates "history" from "fiction") by showing, among other things, that the privileged term in the opposition in fact depends upon its "other," and that the superiority of one term to the other is built into the decision that this is a distinction that makes a difference. Third, deconstruction shatters totalities by deconstructing the "identity," the shadowy presence, which they claim to represent. Fourth, and—for our purposes, although not by any means for all purposes—finally, deconstruction grants interpreters permission to interact with texts in ways that we are not at all accustomed to; deconstruction suggests to us that there are no unnatural acts of textual intercourse.

These effects strike at the heart of the dominant practices of biblical criticism in the academy and, usually, in the church. Both of these institutions reflect and reproduce the assumption that biblical interpretation is properly the domain of an elite group of authorized interpreters; the principal fields of biblical interpretation depend on the binary oppositions of professor/student and minister/laity. These same privileged interpreters claim to reproduce faithfully the "meaning" or "message" of the text they are interpreting. Perhaps they deliver to us the "voice of Jesus" or the theology of Paul, as though Jesus predictably spoke only in ways that we can now authenticate, or as though Paul deployed theological claims according to a plan we can confidently trace in retrospect. And one may not become one of these institutionally authorized interpreters without having adopted the rules concerning what one may and may not say in the respective biblical-historical and ecclesiastical discourses.

If the deconstructors are right, however, all these aspects of our biblical interpretation industry are intensely problematic. Yet these problematic assumptions provide the marks by which we recognize our legitimate interpreters; what are we to do if we can no longer adhere to the standards and criteria of legitimacy that have long sustained the discipline of biblical studies? What would it mean for postmodern, deconstructive biblicists to inhabit the academy and the church in the way that deconstructive philosophers and literary critics inhabit their domains?

First, the presence of deconstructive biblicists in the academy and the church will mean abandoning the illusion that there is something behind or within the biblical texts that we might get at by way of sufficient research or the right method. We will have to distance ourselves from most of the metaphors for interpretation that we have woven into our disciplinary identities; no longer will we argue over whether the text is a window through which we look into the past, or a mirror in which we see only our own reflection. We will not try to locate the world *behind* the text, or the world *in* the text, or the world *in front of* the text. We will not talk about extracting meaning from the text. We will explain the title we bear—"exegete"—not from the (misleading) etymology of "leading [meaning] out" (as though it were derived from *exagō*, "to lead out") of a text; instead we will point out that the epithet *exēgētēs* (from *exēgeomai*), was typically applied to a leader or advisor (an ancient Greek exegete who specialized in interpretation was usually an expounder of oracles and dreams). Where modern critics delve into the text to get something out of it, we will now acknowledge that meaning—to the extent that there is such a thing—does not inhere in a text any more than it might inhere in a dream (where would it go when you wake up?). Meaning is what we make of texts, not an ingredient in texts.

At the same time, we will be obliged to recognize that academically trained interpreters do not hold exclusive rights to legitimacy in the field of biblical interpretation. This is a lesson that all ought to have learned long ago from the countless varieties of biblical interpretation that have thrived apart from academic authorization. To cite but one politically loaded example, the profound interpretive tradition of biblical exposition in the African-American churches should remind us that our process of academic accreditation was devised by and for a specific social caste, and any system of legitimation that arises from and caters to that caste (remember how few African-American scholars have been admitted into the academy even today, and how recently the doors have been opened to them) can hardly pretend to rest on "universal" or "natural" foundations. If academic interpreters want to talk about "legitimacy" in general, they will have to account for many more sorts of interpretation than they habitually do; if they want to stay within the limits they have constructed for their discipline, they will have to concede their irrelevance to parties that do not observe the same ascetic interpretive regime.

Just as deconstructive reading will no longer allow a simple binary opposition separating the legitimate interpreters (academically trained scholars and clerics) from those who are not authorized to interpret (nonexperts, the laity), it will likewise undermine the hitherto sacred distinction between historical interpretation and all other sorts. Where deconstructive insights flourish, the boundary between history and fiction—already hard to pinpoint—will become less and less clear. The same principle applies to the distinctions between historical interpretation and theological, political, literary, feminist, or psychological interpretation, distinctions that currently underwrite the disciplinary identity of biblical studies. Whereas historians are accustomed to setting the limits for all other uses of the Bible ("You may say this, but not that"), they will have to resign themselves to representing just one interpretive interest in the clamor of the hermeneutical boardwalk.

At this point in the chapter, we can think of the interpretive situation in a certain (deconstructive) way. The authority of classical historical criticism depends on the existence of an "original," a "real history," which historical criticism has a privileged method for discovering. Of course, there are various "originals" at stake in various brands of historical criticism: the original words and deeds of biblical personages (in historical Jesus research, for example); the original meanings of the biblical words (in historical philology); the original texts of the Bible (in textual criticism); the original identities and intentions of the writers; the original social contexts for biblical events and for the composition and compilation of biblical writings; and so on. If we displace the notion of "the original" from its position as biblical interpretation's center of gravity, however, the entire operation begins to reel in quite disconcerting ways.

For example, what would it mean to have ascertained, beyond any historical doubt, the original identity, intentions, and social context of Habakkuk? We have seen that the very notion of an identity effaces the multiplicity that always haunts the site of any putative unity; our newly defined, unified Habakkuk would have to be more predictable and blander than the "original"—otherwise we could not predict with assurance what he might have said. (If we posited an unpredictable Habakkuk, we could not be certain that we had defined him.) Our reconstructed social setting will have ignored or oversimplified countless social interactions that will have seemed crucially important to their participants. Our account of Habakkuk's intentions will obviously omit such irrelevant concerns as Habakkuk's intent to finish this or that page before the Sabbath—but then we must explain what criterion we use to judge any of Habakkuk's intentions "irrelevant." Or we must include all of Habakkuk's intentions, on the off chance that one that appears irrelevant to us may seem more meaningful to other interpreters (remember Nietzsche's umbrella). If we devote even a few minutes to considering the complexity of these matters, we recognize that we are never in a position to recapture "the original" of any of these categories.

We ought not be surprised or disappointed by this, however. The very notion of "the original" does not stand up to careful scrutiny. There is, after all, no original thing that is not itself constituted by unoriginal ingredients. The original is a lot like the proper name, which—as we saw above—never escapes the flux of signification and representation. Indeed, we produce what we have called "original" identities, intentions, social contexts, and the like, when we feel a need for them, but they were not lurking in some immaterial zone of originality awaiting our summons. Indeed, it seems much more plausible to let go of the desire to capture Habakkuk in an "original" identity description (in other words, to admit that even "the original Habakkuk," Habakkuk as he really was, was an improvised affair, continually made up as he went along, which or who produced not *one identity* but various versions of Habakkuk) than to try to pin down one account of the prophet and accord it the privilege of bearing the title "the original Habakkuk." "The original" of which we speak is never itself the original, but is our version of an "[non]original" that does not exist as such apart from our demand for such an original.

These manufactured "originals"—which, as if to proclaim their belatedness, all always differ from the "originals" that other interpreters manufacture for the "same" referent—will manifestly not accomplish the work that classical historical critics demand of them. A manufactured "original" cannot add to a historian's interpretation any authority that the interpretation lacked at the outset, and historians are surely in an odd position if they demand that other interpreters (theologians, for example) use these "originals" as the guarantee that their interpretations are valid. Just which representation of the nonexistent original ought an interpreter rely on?

If, on the other hand, all we have are versions of some text/person/social setting—"versions" both in the sense of "particular interpretations" and in the etymological or medical sense of "turnings, rotations"—then the historian's version of a biblical text has no inherently greater claim to authority than does any other version. This does not, of course, mean that all versions are equal; they all differ. This simply means that we cannot short-circuit our responsibility to exercise the spiritual gift of discernment by conceding that an interpretation that is adorned with academic credentials and access to publishing facilities is automatically superior. We are now free to, and obliged to, recognize that our Grandma may produce a sounder interpretation of a psalm than does a Reverend Professor. If she wants to make a claim about the historical likelihood of one or another event, we will probably assay her claim with help from those who have immersed their lives in judging such claims. If, on the other hand, she wants to produce a version of the text that does not suffer from the modern anxiety to legitimate interpretation with reference to history, then we may resort to other means of discerning the legitimacy of her claim.

When postmodern biblical criticism takes its cues from deconstruction, then countless different things may happen, but the resulting interpretations are never indifferent.

A quick example may spice up this dry discourse: As I suggested above, a deconstructive reader begins an interpretation by noticing a point that a conventional reading of the text would highlight; the deconstructor then displaces the conventional reading by noticing a textual or theoretical ambiguity that the conventional reading suppresses. Derrida, for example, has called attention to terms like "supplement," which may indicate either an additional amount that brings a quantity to wholeness (such as the vitamin supplements we may take to ensure that we get enough nourishment) or an amount over and above wholeness (such as the supplementary reading that teachers assign beyond the required reading). Among the other terms to which Derrida has devoted persistent attention is the "signature"—a signifier whose importance depends upon its exclusive, unambiguous relation to its signified (the identity of the signer).

What is a signature? That is, what counts as a signature—in what contexts does a signature make a difference? A mark is counted as a signature (rather than, say, simply "writing one's name" or "a blurry line") when it has the force of a representation of an absent assent. It stands in for a signator who is not present, who would presumably say, "I testify to this," if she were present. In order for a signature to have this effect, it must be unique to the individual whom it represents. If I had a friend named Annamaria Katrina Magdalena Adam and we both signed our names with identical signatures,

our signatures would have lost their effect. It would be impossible to determine whether *I* were withdrawing money from *her* bank account, or whether *she* were contracting to teach *my* courses. An individual's signature must be different from other signatures in order to be effectual.

At the same time, a signature must always be reproducible. It must not be so very distinctive that one could not reproduce it on each check one writes, on each contract one signs. Moreover, the signature should be recognizable, because a signature whose ownership is ambiguous is useless. A signature that is unique in every respect is as useless as a shared signature; we need to compare two (or more) instances of a signature to ascertain the authenticity of the signature. Indeed, the signature ought not be too predictable in any respect, lest it be too easily counterfeited; thus the signature should always be distinct from other instances of the signature, but even more from every other signature. In order for the economy of signatures to function properly, then, one's signed name should be different from all other signed names and should be distinct from other occurrences of one's signature only in indifferent ways. A proper signature, one that abides by these rules, marks its site (a check, a painting, an affidavit, a letter) as authentic.

We have already discussed one difficulty with this sort of reasoning. The representative signifier (be it proper name or signature) stands in for the (absent) signified signator only on the condition that there is an effective distinction between the two: The proper name is not the individual; the signature remains effective in the absence of the signator. This oddity only begins the problems with signatures, however; you may have guessed at some of the further problems while you were reading the last paragraph.

First, then, the signature stands in for the signator; but only if the alleged signator actually signed her name. If a friend signs my name, I am not bound by her action; if a stranger signs my name, not only am I not bound by the stranger's action, but the stranger violates various laws. The signature itself, however, does not reveal who signed it. So, for example, Derrida ends one of his essays ("Signature Event Context") with his signature; but in a subsequent essay ("Limited Inc abc . . .") he claims that the signature in question was not "from his hand" (p. 33). The mark in question seems to say, "J. Derrida"; but in a remark to the side of the alleged signature, someone with the initials "J. D." claims to have counterfeited his own signature ("Signature," p. 21). Whatever the status of the mark in question, whatever the possibility or ethics of forging one's own signature, this case points clearly to the signature's awkward situation: Although the signature needs to function apart from its signator, it is not self-authenticating. A signature is incomplete without the presence of a signator (what would be the status of something that seems to be a signature, but of which no one claimed or admitted to be the signator?).

The signature also suffers from the fact that its principal characteristics—that it be repeatable and not self-identical—clearly permit the possibility that an adept forger may sign another's signature. Indeed, when we recall that postmodern thinkers may question the notion of a unified self-identical person, we are tempted to observe that every signature is a forgery. The A.K.M. Adam who signs a check this morning is not the same person as the A.K.M. Adam who deposited a check last week (who, in turn, is far from being the same person who opened the account several years ago). Or, to put matters more accurately, no signature is more authentic than any other, because none can effect the desired connection between signifier and signified, the self-presence that signatures (fraudulently) represent.

In short, we use the signature to overcome the problem of absence; we establish a whole network of vital social practices on the premise that the signature binds a mark on a page to the self-identical individual. The connection still slips away, however; the signature falls down on the job, leaving us with just as much ambiguity and uncertainty as ever.

This phenomenon is nowhere better illustrated than in the study of the Pauline epistles of the New Testament. Commentators on Paul's letters would have us believe that the single most pressing question they face is the question of authenticity—did Paul actually write this or that letter? Even studies of letters that are almost universally agreed to be Pauline (say, Romans and Galatians) commonly address the question of the letter's authenticity or inauthenticity; C.E.B. Cranfield opens his monumental commentary on the letter to the Romans by raising the authenticity question on the first page. A commentator's approach to the question of authorship decisively influences her interpretation of a given letter. Scholars claim that the authentic letters belong to the context of Paul's own ministry; they come from the fifties and early sixties of the first century, and they express Paul's own character. The *in*authentic letters supposedly come from a later period; they are reckoned derivative and imitative, not original (as Paul's letters are). Even scholars who dissent from these assumptions are so sensitive about this issue that they commonly treat letters whose authenticity is still debated (Colossians and 2 Thessalonians, for instance) as though these letters were known to be inauthentic, in order that they might base their interpretations on the firm foundation of authentically Pauline letters. The seal of authenticity stamps the undoubtedly Pauline letters and cancels the inauthentic deutero-Pauline epistles.

The question of authenticity is not exclusively a contemporary problem. Even the New Testament testifies to the ambiguities of identity and authorship. Second Thessalonians (itself a letter whose authenticity is debated) concerns the appropriate reaction to another letter, which 2 Thessalonians claims is a forgery: "As to the coming of our Lord Jesus Christ and our being gathered together to him, we beg you, brothers and sisters, not to be quickly shaken in mind or alarmed, either by spirit or by word or by letter, *as though from us*, to the effect that the Lord is already here" (2 Thess. 2:1f.). A simple reading of the letter suggests that Paul writes to Thessalonica to prevent the congregation there from falling prey to a forgery that claims Pauline authorship, which teaches "that the Lord is already here"; but this simple reading also entails certain problems.

For example, 2 Thessalonians counters the false letter's Lord-is-here eschatology by reminding the Thessalonians what the author says that he taught them while he was present among them, that there will be unambiguous signs (signifiers) before the day of the Lord. There will be rebellion, and the lawless one will be revealed, before Jesus comes to destroy the lawless one with his breath. If Paul wrote 2 Thessalonians, however, he seems to be contradicting his teaching in 1 Thessalonians, where he says that the Thessalonians know very well that the Lord will come suddenly. Biblical scholars see this as a contradiction; they assume that Paul (whom we know as a unified individual identity) could not say both things.

Another problem with the simple reading is that 2 Thessalonians uses much of the same vocabulary that 1 Thessalonians uses. While, once again, the simple explanation might be that the same author wrote both letters, Pauline scholars suspect that so many of the same words appear in 2 Thessalonians that it must be a conscious *imitation* of 1 Thessalonians. The antiauthenticity party deems the case against 2 Thessalonians' vocabulary all the more convincing, because the author of 2 Thessalonians uses these same words with meanings different from the meanings they bore in 1 Thessalonians. (I will call this writer "Poly," for many identities have been ascribed to this shadow of Paul's.) Poly is, as it were, forging Paul's signature vocabulary. The vocabulary is both too similar and too different to convince some critics.

The final argument that 2 Thessalonians is not authentically Pauline rests on another signature. In verse 3:17, the letter reads, "I, Paul, write this greeting with my own hand. This is the mark in every letter of mine; it is the way I write." According to Pauline scholars, Poly doth protest too much; this heavy emphasis on Paul's own handwriting suggests not so much that the apostle himself is signing the letter as that Poly, in a bold stroke, is calling attention to the signature in an effort to create the impression that it is in fact Paul's handwriting. Given this clue, some critics equate the "false letter" of 2:1 with 1 Thessalonians; they argue that the forger seeks to establish 2 Thessalonians' deferred eschatology, so the forger displaces the earlier authentic Pauline letter with the forged 2 Thessalonians.

Poly, knowing the duplicity of signatures, simply enacts a strikingly Derridean rhetorical ploy. The forger plays on the ambiguity of the signifying signature to blur the distinction between his or her identity and Paul's identity, to exclude Paul from his own proper name. "Where Paul was, I will be."

If we check the undisputed Pauline letters to see whether the real Paul actually does make his mark in every letter he writes, signing his name with his own hand, we find that this is very nearly true. First Corinthians closes with exactly the same words that begin 2 Thess. 3:17: "I, Paul, write this greeting with my own hand" (16:21). So likewise Galatians: "See what large letters I make when I am writing in my own hand" (6:11). And Paul assures Philemon, "I, Paul, am writing this with my own hand" (19).

These undisputed testimonials would incline one to think that Paul characteristically adds solemn asseverations of his authentic signature; but once again, things are not so simple. Colossians, a letter whose authenticity is uncertain, also calls attention to its signature, once again using the same words as 1 Corinthians and 2 Thessalonians: "I, Paul, write this greeting with my own hand" (4:18). Is Colossians also Poly's work? Do the scholars who reject the 2 Thessalonians signature formula suppose that two forgers independently chose the same fraudulent claim to shore up their pseudonymous letters, or that one forger stole the idea from another?

One may well suppose that Poly had a collection of Pauline letters at hand when composing 2 Thessalonians; indeed, the note that Paul (or Poly) signs every letter this way might suggest that Poly has checked up on Paul's habit (Paul does not make this point in any other letter). If we adopt this position, we ought to reexamine our certainty that 1 Corinthians, Galatians, and Philemon are authentic; perhaps Poly, the artful forger who specializes in reproducing Paul's epistolary style, has slipped several fakes past the handwriting experts. Or perhaps the original Paul really did write all of the letters we are discussing.

Of course, one of the curiosities of the whole debate is that in every existing edition of 2 Thessalonians, the crucial claim in 3:17 that the letter is Paul's own handwriting is patently false; there exists no copy of 2 Thessalonians in Paul's writing (or Poly's, for that matter). Indeed, in most copies of 2 Thessalonians, these words are not only not written with Paul's own hand, they are not handwritten at all, but typeset by an anonymous compositor (not Paul nor Poly either). Here is a case where the words of the Bible are demonstrably erroneous. The words might have been true in their original setting if the letter were authentically Pauline—but then again, as we have seen, they might not.

So, is 2 Thessalonians an authentic Pauline letter? Once we have taken this deconstructive tour through Pauline criticism, the question and the binary opposition it presupposes—authentic/inauthentic, with the first term the privileged, originary partner—seem rather different. We have seen that the same bits of evidence work on both sides of the argument. The diction is plausibly Pauline—but perhaps too Pauline, or not quite Pauline enough (and therefore Polyne). Paul was concerned that a forged letter might mislead the Thessalonian congregation, or Poly feared that the authentic letter might mislead them, that the forgery might not convince them. The signature is an understandable precaution taken in light of a fear of forgery, or it seems like an excessive effort to authenticate the letter by a bold imitator ("You yourselves know how you ought to imitate us," Paul [or Poly] says at 2 Thess. 3:7, but this is probably not what Paul would have had in mind). In a word, the question is undecidable; it will not be settled by an appeal to the "evidence," because the evidence is double minded, duplicitous.

We need not stop wondering who wrote 2 Thessalonians, and what the author meant by the "false letter," but we do need to recuperate from our captivity to undecidable questions like this one. By displacing the question of authenticity from its central importance, we introduce a degree of looseness (Derrida calls this "play") into our interpretations; we no longer have a rigid commitment to a single foundation (a foundation that, as we have seen, may not sustain the weight we impose on it). The question of why we need to pin down the identity of an author, of what difference "authenticity" makes, will be as prominent to us as will be the question of who wrote what.

This point gives the lie to criticisms that claim that deconstruction is inherently apolitical. A deconstructive critical practice displaces the interpretive laws that separate "political" from "scientific" or "scholarly" interests. While some deconstructive interpreters have chosen not to undertake obviously political investigations, deconstruction has played an important role in persuading many readers that all interpretation is political (and all politics is, in a certain way, hermeneutical). Beginning deconstructors who want to pursue outlandish interpretations while maintaining strong political commitments need to develop alternative practices of interpretation, rather than simply deconstructing people's ideas (What if the international meetings of biblical scholarship took place in the abandoned row houses of urban slums, instead of in hotels and convention centers?). Instead of rendering the house of biblical criticism uninhabitable, deconstruction has changed our understanding of what it means to live someplace. We can continue to dwell in the domain of academic biblical criticism, in a certain way, but we will pursue our interpretations *differently*.

Further Reading

Derrida's work on signatures in "Signature Event Context" and "Limited Inc. abc" can most easily be consulted in *Limited Inc* (Evanston, Ill.: Northwestern Univ. Press, 1988), which concludes with an interview that should help readers tangle with deconstruction. *Semeia* 23 (1982) is dedicated to Derrida and his relevance to biblical studies; the articles therein are helpful introductions to Derrida, as are Christopher Norris's books *Derrida* (Cambridge: Harvard Univ. Press, 1987) and *Deconstruction: Theory and Practice* (New York: Methuen, 1982), Jonathan Culler's *On Deconstruction* (Ithaca, N.Y.: Cornell Univ. Press), Mark Taylor's article, "Deconstruction: What's the Difference" (*Soundings* 66 [1983]: 387–403), and Edward Greenstein's "Deconstruction and Biblical Narrative" (*Prooftexts* 21:4 [1989]). Paul de Man's "The Rhetoric of Blindness" in *Blindness and Insight*, 2d ed. (Minneapolis: Univ. of Minnesota Press, 1983), 102–41, is another excellent preparation for entering the domain of deconstructive discourse.

There is no simple entry point into Derrida's writing, although such fundamental texts as "Structure, Sign, and Play in the Discourse of the Human Sciences" in *Writing and Difference*, trans. Alan Bass (Chicago: Univ. of Chicago Press, 1978), 278–93, "Différance," and "White Mythology" in *Margins of Philosophy*, trans. Alan Bass (Chicago: Univ. of Chicago Press, 1982), 1–27, 207–72, address an audience of readers whom Derrida did not expect to be already familiar with his work. His "Letter to a Japanese Friend"—collected with numerous other valuable Derridean essays into *A Derrida Reader: Between the Blinds*, ed. Peggy Kamuf (New York: Columbia Univ. Press, 1991)—discusses what "deconstruction" might be. *Positions*, trans. Alan Bass (Chicago: Univ. of Chicago Press, 1981)—which comprises a number of interviews—may also be a useful starting point. Derrida collaborated with Geoff Bennington on a work that both summarized Derrida's thought thus far and extended his work beyond the limits of the summary: *Jacques Derrida: Derridabase/Circumf-essions* (Chicago: Univ. of Chicago Press, 1993). I have especially enjoyed his "No Apocalypse, Not Now" (*diacritics* 14 [1984]: 20–31).

Stephen Moore offers a characteristically sharp and valuable section on Derrida in *Literary Criticism and the Gospels*. Moore has edited a *Semeia* volume that displays some of the impact that Derridean deconstruction has had on biblical studies: "Poststructuralism as Exegesis," in *Semeia* 54 (1991); see also "Poststructural Criticism of the Bible: Text/History/Discourse" in *Semeia* 51 (1990). Moore undertakes further Derridean biblical interpretation in *Mark and Luke in Poststructuralist Perspective* (New Haven: Yale Univ. Press, 1991), and *Poststructuralism and the New Testament: Derrida and Foucault at the Foot of the Cross* (Minneapolis: Fortress Press, 1994).

3
Political Criticism: Ideologies and Their Discontents

In the first chapter I suggested that "demystifying" bears a strong kinship to distinctively modern interpretive practices. This should not be surprising; readers who undertake political criticism are typically troubled by particular conditions of human existence, conditions of poverty and oppression that the critics would not want to dissolve into "textuality" or "theory." When politically sensitive readers want to take seriously the real material conditions of various people's lives, they often appeal to the conclusions of historical criticism without hesitation. Yet this is usually historical criticism with a difference. Whereas their more conventional colleagues simply rely on the hammer and nails that the familiar (European-American) construction technique calls for, political critics will enter the discourse with a different box of analytical tools. They will select a variety of nontraditional interpretive implements to accent the relation of a text to particular oppressed groups. To the extent that political critics leave questions about their definitions of "history" or "unified subjects" unanswered, they frequently adopt modern interpretive habits. But because modern interpreters present their conclusions as the objective results of scientific investigation, we can tentatively label some readers as postmodern political interpreters on the basis of their resistance to objectivity, their explicit advocacy of political ends, and their suspicion of biblical texts' (and interpreters') concealed ideological interests.

We see how this delicate balancing act works out in the cases of Michel Foucault (on one hand) and the "New Historicism" (on the other). Foucault produced a series of historical studies that appear no more revolutionary than any other scholarly works on the history of hospitals, or of prisons; yet while Foucault made many of the correct historical moves (consulting aged primary sources, drawing on the testimony of eyewitnesses, and so on), his conclusions were startlingly out of step with conventional histories. Most historians add detail to the stories we tell about the past, or correct the stories that other historians have told—that is, they describe the world. Foucault wrote to change the world by telling an ostensibly objective story with rhetorical devices designed to startle, sometimes horrify the reader. Whereas historians typically seek the roots of events and ideas in earlier events and ideas, tying them together in a long causal chain, Foucault seeks out discontinuities, breaks in the chain, to undermine the notion that "sameness" persists in a body or institution over time. The modern prison is not the same kind of institution as the dungeons or the public gallows, although theorists tend to treat them as different links in the chain we call "penal theory." The discourses that circulate about the gallows (on one hand) and the modern prison (on the other hand) involve different goals, different means toward those goals, different sets of terms, different definitions of who counts as an expert, and so on. If one wants to maintain that public hanging and modern imprisonment are both part of the same discourse of penal theory, then one must explain why the few discursive similarities between these two systems outweigh a tremendous variety of differences.

Foucault uses the tools with which historiography constructs its grand theoretical edifices to destabilize the monuments of historiography, so that they collapse of their own weight. When Foucault uses these ancient and obscure sources, archival records, medical and technical histories, he uses them in ways that modern historians deem awkward and unsafe, in order to call into question the whole historical how-to book.

The "New Historicism" is another intellectual current that muddies any distinction between modern and postmodern political criticism. Modern "historicists" believe that scholars may not be able finally to attain objectivity, but that students of history are obliged to strive for objectivity nonetheless. These "old" historicists submit that events and ideas are of a piece with their historical moment, so that one must understand the prevalent assumptions of a given historical moment in order to understand a text from that moment. They usually take aspects of the texts as reflections of these prevalent ideas; they interpret a text on the basis of its historical context. New (postmodern) Historicists typically regard objectivity as a charade through and through; they are partisan and they are unashamed. They stipulate that any contemporary description of a past moment draws on various clues from the time of that past moment and then compounds those clues from the past with an assortment of modern assumptions about "what that moment must have been like." Thus the New Historicists show that the context that *modern* (*not* New) historicists posit for a given work will actually reflect not only the prevalent ideas of the past historical moment, but also, in concealed form, the prevalent assumptions of the historicist's own day. The New Historicists generally seek more thoroughly to situate the texts they study in the competing cultural impulses and the practices of the everyday life of their texts' times, and they are more candid about the role of their own imaginative constructions.

New Historicists also resist the "text/context" binary opposition; texts are part of their context, and the historical context is woven into the text, so that any text we find may be as much an act of subversive resistance to the prevalent ideas of the time as it is a sign of the times. Even more, texts may be internally contested; the text may present the prevalent ideas, but it may be resisting the prevalent ideology at the same time. In the same way, literary texts do not simply subsist as part of a canon of great books that floats above the grubby particularities of social existence; writers compose literary texts within certain material, political, and cultural circumstances. A New Historicist might point out that the former way of thinking about literary texts assumed that great books automatically shared the great ideas (read: dominant ideology) of their culture; as a result, one might never imagine that writers were paid, or had unpopular views, or were ambivalent about the great ideas, or acted out of partisan political motives. In this sense, the New Historicism is arguably truer to history than its older precedents, because it is highly likely that writers did behave and think more along the ways New Historicists suggest than in the ethereal, ideal ways implicit in older historicism.

Criticism that develops from the work of Foucault, from the New Historicism, and from many other approaches that we can collect under the banner of political criticism, will develop in ways that depend to a great extent on the interpreter's definition of "ideology." Collections of diverse definitions now adorn many books and articles, but I will concentrate here on three possibilities: The first stresses the falsity of ideology; the second stresses the generality of ideology; and the third stresses the work of ideology. The former comes from Marx and Engels's analyses of political ideology; the latter two come more from the response to the Marxist definition.

Some critics define "ideology" starting from the Marxist conviction that people put up with oppressive conditions in part because the social practices that dominate their lives express a misleading justification of their situation. On this account—characteristic of most of Marx's own writing—the means of production, the character of class relations, and the vocabulary of political life all constitute an enacted description of "how things are." That description underwrites the oppressive circumstances that undermine the inclination to resist. This sort of ideology is always deceptive. It results from the contradictions that inhere in the social and economic processes, such that (in order to think coherently at all) people must attribute coherence to an incoherent world. When an abused spouse excuses the abuser's brutality by saying, "It's for my own good," and when a laborer explains low wages by saying, "That's all my abilities are worth," they are rationalizing their oppressions in terms that their oppressors have taught them. Marx referred to this as "false consciousness."

Another group of interpreters treats "ideology" as any set of political goals and assumptions, more or less synonymous with a "political agenda." Most casual English speakers use the term this way; they attribute a columnist's bitter invective to her conservative *ideology*. In this usage, "ideology" is more flexible than in the former; we need not subscribe to a dichotomy between "false consciousness" and an enlightened, truly conscious rejection of ideology. At the same time, when we use the term this way, we risk allowing it to become redundant. If everyone has an ideology, then the term "ideology" often ends up meaning nothing other than "opinion" or "conviction." Moreover, the term tends to float free from the Marxist emphasis on material social conditions, which emphasis helps make the term valuable. This use of "ideology" is more characteristic of the opponents of ideological criticism than of its exponents.

A third body of readers finds the first ("false consciousness") definition of "ideology" too limiting, and the second ("political agenda") definition too idealistic and vague. These critics define an "ideology" as a description of all the social interactions that ascribe "significance" to our behavior. They recognize the value of Marx's insight into the ideological component of oppression, but they go on to use the term not only for cases of "false consciousness," but as a condition for the possibility of all consciousness. Our capacity to produce meaning from experience comes not from an innate faculty, but from our assimilation of socially produced assumptions. These assumptions often oppress many participants in a society, but certain ideological assumptions may have liberating effects (the assumption that human beings have innate "rights," for example).

Ideological critics in biblical interpretation have mostly oscillated between the first (false consciousness) and third (social production of meaning) uses of "ideology," with an emphasis falling on the first. Most of the prominent ideological-critical biblical scholars have stressed that the biblical writings reflect and reproduce the false consciousness of oppressed groups. They argue that dominant social groups, which produced and saved biblical texts, shaped these texts to correspond to the dominant

48

groups' class interests. This claim, uncomfortably, involves the ideological critics in a distinctly modern philosophical position, whereby the critics occupy a privileged site of knowledge and truth, and the texts they survey contain ideological errors. (A more postmodern tack would acknowledge that all composition and interpretation involve ideology, and that biblical texts can easily be construed in ways that reinforce structures that oppress the lower classes.) "Ideology" is a highly fluid term, however, and readers should keep a weather eye on what work it seems to be doing in any given source.

The most familiar ideological criticism of the Bible is feminist criticism; feminists in America can look back with admiration to such foremothers as Sarah Grimké and Elizabeth Cady Stanton. Feminist readers produce a wide variety of ideological-critical readings: they call our attention to the explicitly horrifying stories about women in the Bible (the raped and dismembered concubine of Judges 19 is perhaps the most outrageous victim, although she has many sisters), to the ways women are implicitly and explicitly relegated to secondary status, and to the possible sources for resisting patriarchal domination (to cite but a few feminist reading strategies).

Some feminist scholars concentrate on criticizing the androcentric, patriarchal ideology that they find in the Bible. They point out that biblical texts deal principally with men and only secondarily with women, as if to say that men's lives constitute the important part of everyday life and that women's lives are important only to the extent that women interrupt the flow of men's experience. Likewise, they point out, biblical texts typically assume that leadership and public activity belong to men. Moreover, the relatively few women characters in the Bible include a disproportionate number whose importance is summed up by their sexual status: virgins, concubines, wives, prostitutes, victims of rape and other sexual violence, sacrificial offerings, child bearers (Phyllis Trible named these "texts of terror"). Feminist criticism directs attention to the problems of regarding a text as sacred that can, for instance, narrate the story of a drunken father impregnating his two young daughters (and place the responsibility for this on the daughters) without wincing. How are feminist interpreters to make sense of the Bible when it presupposes and explicitly highlights a patriarchal ideology?

Feminist scholars also expose the patriarchal assumptions under which biblical scholarship is typically conducted (Elisabeth Schüssler Fiorenza stands out among these critics). One obvious indicator of this phenomenon is the modifier "feminist"; a critic who devotes considerable time to the situation of women in the Bible will be called a "feminist critic," but another who devotes her attention to the preponderant male-dominated texts is not known as a "masculinist critic." A classic instance of critical androcentrism concerns the "greetings" section of Romans. Interpreters have long argued that the "Junia," whom Paul describes as "prominent among the apostles," must be a shortened form of "Junias" or "Julianus," because a woman could not have been a prominent apostle (this despite the fact that Junia was a common name for Roman women and is unknown as a name for a man). This problem is especially challenging because many feminist scholars want to make claims about the real historical setting of ancient Israel or nascent Christianity, but are limited by modern historians' reluctance to admit that their interpretive methods are complicit with patriarchal androcentrism.

While feminist criticism is most prominent among the political criticisms, an increasing number of critics concentrate on the ways the Bible reflects class conflict and class interests. These interpreters generally reflect a Marxism mediated to American critical circles via Fredric Jameson and British scholars Raymond Williams and (especially) Terry Eagleton. Their pioneer is Norman Gottwald, who published his monumental *The Tribes of Yahweh* in 1979.

Ideological critics (you may notice that readers who attend to the political and economic aspects of biblical ideology are "ideological critics," whereas those who pay attention to patriarchal ideology are "feminist critics") point out that the biblical narratives were produced in particular social or economic settings, but that interpreters commonly ignore the likelihood that these texts served ideological functions relative to their setting. Just as feminist interpreters locate patriarchally oppressive biblical texts, ideological critics stress the oppressive (or liberatory) ideological content of the Bible. They point out that texts that were compiled at about the time Israel changed from a tribal confederation to a monarchical state bear the marks of that transition—marks either of the dominant social class's efforts to legitimate its newfound centralized power, or of the marginalized groups' resistance to the new power structure. Because the dominant social classes were in the position to promulgate and preserve texts, there is much in the Bible that serves oppressive interests.

One way ideological critics discern the oppressive aspects of texts involves attending to a Marxist emphasis on the mode of production prevalent at the time of the text's composition. The period during which the biblical texts were written and compiled saw conflicts and transitions among various modes of production; if Gottwald is right, the Israelite conquest of Canaan provides the most striking example of these conflicts. Canaan (and the people who gathered together under the name of "Israel") had long been dominated by a feudal "tributary" (or "Asiatic") mode of production, in which a vast peasant class farmed for subsistence and paid heavy tributes to local and regional rulers. At the time described by the books of Joshua and Judges, these peasants launched a haphazard revolution that eventually succeeded in overcoming most of the indigenous Canaanite lords in the name of a people's movement called Israel, which claimed the favor of a god named YHWH. While the texts talk about the wars between Israelites and Canaanites, between the God of Israel and the gods of the Canaanites and Philistines, ideological critics point to the conflict between the tributary mode of production and Israel's policy of locating production within the more or less autonomous extended family unit of the "tribe."

The ideological critics also point to the effects of critics' own ideologies; that is, they may point out the ways in which biblical critics' social and economic location has determined their interpretations. They may note that one can only begin to think in grand abstractions (like "humanity" or "history") and to insist on "objectivity" when one is freed from the necessity of scrabbling for one's sustenance and struggling for political change. This situates modern historical inquiry as a fundamentally bourgeois phenomenon that underwrites its own authority by ignoring non-bourgeois voices (who, after all, have not attained the requisite expertise at the appropriate academies). Thus modern historical criticism reproduces its own ideological characteristics and presses them upon others by holding up bourgeois interpreters as privileged judges of biblical interpretation. At the same time, the interpreters themselves identify as most important not the class struggle reflected in the texts but the abstract, existential religious themes. Biblical ideological critics aim at demystifying the "religious" aura of the Bible and relocating the Bible as a site of and a tool in ideological conflict. They reveal the ideological cracks that have been plastered over with the façade of ideologically suspect spirituality; they uncover and stress the texts that may be useful in countering oppressive structures; and they attack the pervasive ideological bias of the discipline of biblical studies.

Ideological criticism extends beyond the critique of patriarchal and class structures, however. Biblical studies has recently seen a groundswell of publications and papers on the impact of racial ideology on interpretation. Although in some cases African-American critics question the ideological soundness of the biblical texts themselves, they have thus far devoted much more energy to ideological problems with specific biblical interpretations and with the discipline of biblical criticism. While biblical texts have been used to support slavery and apartheid, African-American interpreters have (as one may well understand) recognized these as ideologically loaded uses of a text that otherwise provides manifest imperatives to liberation and integration. While scholars have dissected and dismissed the pernicious "Hamitic myth" (that the black races of Africa were accursed when Noah pronounced the curse of slavery on Canaan in Genesis 9) and have shown that the biblical warrants for slavery were misused as justifications of American slavery, they continue to allow the erasure of Africa from biblical geography, of African identity from biblical characters.

Euro-American biblical scholars typically bypass matters such as Moses' race without a word; this is, for the dominant group, a nonissue (and illustrative representations of Moses reveal an image that resembles a standard European physiognomy much more than an African appearance). For readers who do not have the luxury of overlooking questions of racial identity in daily life, the question of Moses' race is a topic of considerable critical interest. Likewise, the typical map of the "biblical world" defines this area as the Mediterranean basin together with Palestine and Mesopotamia; map makers either ignore the African lands that play roles in the Bible, or they relegate them to the inconsequential margins by depicting only a handful of the relevant cities and regions. Few reference works convey the vivid Israelite presence in Ethiopia (where the Elephantine papyri testify to a thriving Israelite colony with its own temple); few Euro-American commentators call their readers' attention to the prospect of the Ethiopian Queen of Sheba judging the world (to which Jesus alludes in Luke 11:31f.).

Finally, some scholars are beginning to criticize the ways in which the Eurocentric historical-critical method of interpretation silences the African-American interpreters who have not had the privilege of academic training in biblical interpretation. While generations of African-American preachers and orators sustained a vital tradition of biblical interpretation, the official documents of academic biblical interpretation disregard these contributions. Most institutions of academic biblical interpretation will offer African Americans who pursue the vocation of academic biblical interpretation a choice: Either they may turn their backs on the interpretive traditions that could well have inspired their interest in biblical studies, or they may isolate themselves from the means of accreditation, employment, and publication. Such an unpalatable choice bespeaks the effects of racial ideology in the supposedly objective domain of academic biblical interpretation.

In all these areas, political criticism of the Bible follows to a great extent the pattern set by modern demystifying. Political critics who rely on metanarratives of emancipation, or who assume that people have some innate human rights, are subject to the antifoundational and detotalizing critiques of other postmodern critical discourses. These modern-leaning political critics will need to come to terms with this awkward vulnerability. They will also need to deal delicately with their tendency to assume that ideologies can abide within texts; chapter 2 suggested that texts do not have a "within" for containing ideologies. Ideology does not lurk concealed between the lines of the texts; rather, the people who inscribe texts, the social groups that preserve texts, and the people and groups that read texts, teach, think, select, and interpret ideologically (that is, their very notions of meaning are subject to many interconnected socially embodied assumptions).

At the same time, when political critics turn their attention to modern interpretive discourses' foundational or totalizing claims, they are undertaking a more clearly postmodern endeavor. They are stripping away the mystifying gauze of supposed objectivity that conceals modern criticism's patriarchal, economic, and racial biases. One might apply the heuristic rule that interpreters who press you to accept their objectivity are probably concealing an ideological aim, whether consciously or unconsciously. Postmodern political critics, on the other hand, will not dodge the accusation that they are pleading a case. So long as modern interpreters claim that the nature of historical argument rules out such "advocacy" in interpretations, there will be postmodern ideological critics who resolutely call attention to the ideological function that "objectivity" serves in modern interpretive discourse.

The most consistently postmodern political critics will eschew claims that their interpretations are true, whereas their opponents' interpretations are "ideological"; they will acknowledge that there is no universal discourse of truth that could support a distinction between my true interpretation and an opponent's ideological interpretation. Instead, these critics will work from a particular local set of truth claims whose cogency they exemplify by committing their lives to them in accordance with Marx's second "Thesis on Feuerbach":

> The question whether objective truth can be attributed
> to human thinking is not a question of theory but is a

> practical question. Man [sic] must prove the truth, that
> is, the reality and power, the this-sidedness of his think-
> ing in practice. The dispute over the reality or nonreal-
> ity of thinking which is isolated from practice is a purely
> scholastic question.

Postmodern ideological critics will continue to point out the ways that dominant social groups' approaches to the Bible produce and reproduce oppressive social relations, but they will also produce counterreadings to contest the prevalent interpretive customs. Such counterreadings rest not upon better research and more objective analysis—thus leaving intact the apparatus with which our dominant culture produces its oppressive readings—but on alternate approaches to interpretation, approaches that more closely reflect the local truths for which the ideological critics stand.

Such a postmodern ideological criticism might approach the domain of biblical studies with the observation that both the Old and New Testaments express an internal contradiction with regard to the basis of the human relation to God. On one hand, God promises to preserve and save people solely on the basis of God's own love: "It was because the LORD loved you and kept the oath that was sworn to your ancestors, that the LORD has brought you out with a mighty hand, and redeemed you from the house of slavery, from the hand of Pharaoh king of Egypt" (Deut. 7:8, alt.), and "The wages of sin is death, but the free gift of God is eternal life in Christ Jesus our Lord" (Rom. 6:23). Passages like these stress the gratuity of God's grace. On the other hand, there is also a strong emphasis on a theology that characterizes the basis of salvation as an (economic) exchange. In the Hebrew Bible, humanity rectifies its relationship with God when men offer God sacrifices, and in the New Testament, humanity is saved when Christ ransoms his sisters and brothers "once for all at the end of the age [removing] sin by the sacrifice of himself" (Heb. 9:26). The difference between these two accounts of how people can rectify their relation to God is neither inconsequential nor ideologically innocent.

The sacrificial system, for example, reproduces a hierarchical social economy that subordinates women and that introduces a medium of exchange by which humanity can, in effect, buy a right standing with God. Of course, numerous passages testify to Israel's horror that one should draw this conclusion. The prophets especially try to suppress the equation of holy offerings with divine bribes. At the same time, the biblical writers persistently define the divine-human relation in terms of appropriate or inappropriate sacrifices and offerings.

The sacrificial economy pushes women to the margins in several ways. First, women are denied access to the mechanics of offering; only male Levites and Aaronites may accede to priesthood. The Bible defines priests in several different ways, but none of these even comes close to permitting women to function as priests in a sacrificial economy. Women may no more be priests than may a man with crushed testicles or a club foot; they interact with the priesthood chiefly as potential sources of defilement.

Second, women of biblical narrative did not typically control possessions suitable for sacrifice. They could not offer sacrifices because they had little to offer. Whatever the condition of women in ancient Palestine may have been, the women in the Bible are typically adjuncts to men. When women need sacrificial cleansing or reconciliation, the Law typically stipulates that her father or husband offers the sacrifices on her behalf. The only woman whom the Bible describes in a situation close to "offering sacrifice" is Hannah, whom the Bible describes going to Shiloh with her husband, Elkanah, to offer the yearly sacrifices, offering her son to God, and bringing livestock and goods to sacrifice at Samuel's dedication as a Nazirite (1 Sam. 1–2). Although the text simply says, "they slaughtered the bull" (1 Sam. 1:25), and the ostensible referents from v. 24 are Hannah and Samuel, Elkanah is presumably still in Shiloh (he does not leave until 2:11). Still, the text notes Elkanah's role as the family's leader; he divides the portions, he allots Hannah a double share, he goes to offer the sacrifice while Hannah is still encumbered with newborn Samuel, and it seems likely that he is included among the "they" who participated in the sacrifice at Samuel's dedication.

Finally, the Bible shows that women are themselves value-laden assets, who are therefore subject to being sacrificed. The Law defines their exchange value, which varies according to their sexual condition; they are the objects of "coveting" in the Decalogue; they are obtained at tremendous personal cost (Abraham's servant gave gold and silver jewelry garments, and ornaments for Rebekah; Jacob labored for Laban fourteen years to "earn" Rachel; David bought Michal at the price of one hundred Philistine's prepuces). One ominous aspect of women's high exchange value is that they then constitute an especially valuable commodity for sacrifice. Jephthah's daughter, for example, figures in her father's story simply as a personified asset: she has no name, and she is described exclusively in economic terms (she is Jephthah's only daughter, and she is a virgin). While she is not the only victim of child sacrifice in the Hebrew Bible (the practice of making sons and daughters "pass through the fire" is attested in several places), her case contrasts starkly with that of Jonathan. Jonathan's father, Saul, makes a vow similar to Jephthah's (1 Sam. 14), but when he indicates his intent to make good his word, the people intercede on Jonathan's behalf, and Saul relents. The biblical writers accord Jonathan a full identity: his own name, his own adventures and relationships, a personality that is not exhausted by defining his sexual status. They do not extend the same narrative status to Jephthah's daughter.

Some might argue that the notion of "sacrifice" is separable from the patriarchal practices that exclude women from the religious leadership, limit women's access to the means of sacrificial atonement, and define women as suitable objects for sacrifice, but the correlation of sacrificial systems and patriarchy (and the market economy) is strong and persistent. The inclination to tinker with the economic machine rather than to look for another model points to a continuity of Israel's sacrificial economy and our own material circumstances (where the market exploits laborers from outside the mainstream of the Euro-American middle class in order to produce more consumer goods for the "developed" world). It will not do simply to shift "women" to the role of cultic authority figures, or to repudiate female sacrifice; the subject-object relations that constitute the sacrificial economy remain intact, and the authorities would identify some other set of "objects" to fill the space "women" left empty. The system, with its proclivities to subordination and scapegoating, remains intact.

Any alternative to the sacrificial economy must address not only the theological model that enacts an exchange between man and God, but also the oppressive gender relations that exchange enforces and the contemporary political and theological situations that make the sacrificial economy seem more or less "natural." One alternative would draw on the biblical texts that stress freedom and trust as the basis for divine-human relations (and, hence, relations between humans). Biblical texts that stress God's lack of interest in sacrifices bespeak one facet of such a "gift" economy; the Bible's stress on charity as a fundamental aspect of Israel's identity is another.

The twin themes of God's gratuitous election of Israel—an election that is not conditional upon sacrificial observance—and of Israel's obligation to care for one another constitute an economy based not on exchange, but on *sharing*. The jubilary theology, which stresses that loans and property transfer are always temporary, always for the needier person's well-being (rather than for the wealthier person's profit), draws on the fundamental notion that God has given Israel life and sustenance freely. Human transactions then mirror God's gracious provision for us instead of reproducing a stark quid pro quo economy, wherein only those who have something to offer can rest comfortably.

This jubilary economy resounds throughout the Hebrew Bible (although not as prominently as the sacrificial economy). Deuteronomy treats widows and orphans—those who have least value in a market economy—as the cardinal example of those for whom faithful Israelites should provide: " 'Cursed be anyone who deprives the alien, the orphan, and the widow of justice.' All the people shall say, 'Amen!' " (27:19). Likewise the prophetic literature is replete with injunctions against abusing the powerless, once again typified as "widows and orphans," as these texts link "righteousness" with "care for the needy." A social system that relied upon these texts would tend to level out social distinctions; although the biblical texts do not envision women's participation in cultic leadership, the impetus to inclusion would be much stronger than is the case in the sacrificial economy. A jubilary economy would undermine the tendency for capital to accumulate in the hands of the few. It would situate the oppressed at the center of social action, rather than relegating them to the margins.

Of course, the biblical jubilary texts are not themselves ideologically innocent. Politically sensitive readers will discern the ways in which the jubilee (for example) continues the ideological distinctions between foreigners and Israelites, perpetuates women's secondary status, and leaves the institution of private property unchallenged; the work of ideological criticism is never done. This does not, of course, diminish the value of ideological criticism, but emphasizes the value of resisting the common tendency to permit comfortable ideologies to prevail unquestioned.

Political criticism undertakes this work of resisting interpretive complacency by showing ways in which our readings depend on our material circumstances. This may take the form of a New Historicism, or of a feminist critique of patriarchy, or of a Marxist jeremiad against bourgeois appropriation of the biblical texts. Many political readers will simply adopt the modern assumptions that ground the interpretations they are resisting; others will seek a different selection of seasonings for their commentaries; they may frequently begin by directing modern demystification against modernity's own assumptions. Where critics subject modern (scientific, specialized, systematized) ideologies to demystification and deconstruction, there we discern a different, postmodern political criticism.

Further Reading

This chapter covers so much terrain that the suggestions for further reading could easily occupy their own bibliographic volume or two; these pages will hardly scratch the surface. Most of the copious literature on political criticism is not, however, especially "postmodern." The following suggestions will cover both the modern and postmodern political criticisms, with mild efforts to estimate the suggested works' postmodernity.

Michel Foucault's work on penal theory, *Discipline and Punish*, trans. Alan Sheridan (New York: Vintage Books, 1979), is probably the best avenue into his longer works, although *The Order of Things* (New York: Vintage Books, 1973) is extremely instructive; the anthologies of his essays and interviews are uneven, but usually quite readable, and they always include provocative insights.

The label "New Historicism" covers many theoretical interests; the literary-critical aspect is well characterized in Jean Howard's essay "The New Historicism in Renaissance Studies" (*English Literary Renaissance* 16 [1986]: 13–43) and in H. Avram Veeser, *The New Historicism* (New York: Routledge, 1989). Hayden White and Dominick LaCapra articulate a New Historicism in a more historiographic vein; see White's *Tropics of Discourse* (Baltimore, Md.: Johns Hopkins Univ. Press, 1978) and LaCapra's *Rethinking Intellectual History* (Ithaca, N.Y.: Cornell Univ. Press, 1983). Roger Dean's *History Making History* (Albany: SUNY Press, 1988) addresses this historiographic New Historicism with an eye to religious studies. Dan Via has drawn on New Historicist studies for his article "New Testament Theology: Historical Event, Literary Text, and the Locus of Revelation" (*Perspectives in Religious Studies* 14 [1992]: 369–88), although his assessment of the New Historicism's import differs from my own. See also Mary Ann Tolbert's contribution, "The Gospel in Greco-Roman Culture," in *The Book and the Text*, ed. Regina Schwartz (Cambridge: Basil Blackwell, 1990). These works are generally categorized as postmodern, although many readers will observe a stark difference between these critics and Foucault (by far the most "post" of them all).

Readers interested in learning more about Marxist approaches to literary works can hardly do better than to read Raymond Williams's *Marxism and Literature* (Oxford: Oxford Univ. Press, 1977) and Terry Eagleton's *Literary Theory* (Minneapolis: Univ. of Minnesota Press, 1983). (Louis Althusser's essay "Ideology and Ideological State Apparatuses" is challenging, but useful; it appears in *Lenin and Philosophy and Other Essays*

[London: New Left Books, 1977].) Marxist interpretation of the Old Testament draws most heavily on Norman Gottwald's work (especially *The Tribes of Yahweh*, 2d ed. [Maryknoll, N.Y.: Orbis, 1981], and *The Hebrew Bible: A Socio-Literary Introduction* [Philadelphia: Fortress Press, 1985]). New Testament interpretation is dominated by critics within the general ambit of liberation theology (such as Fernando Belo's *A Materialist Reading of the Gospel of Mark* (Maryknoll, N.Y.: Orbis, 1981) and Ched Myers's *Binding the Strong Man* (Maryknoll, N.Y.: Orbis, 1988). Michel Clévenot provides a very simple introduction to the subject in *Materialist Approaches to the Bible* (Maryknoll, N.Y.: Orbis, 1985). To the extent that Marxist readings rely on robust confidence in a history that can be scientifically reconstructed and analyzed, they remain modern, but postmodern political criticism still owes a great deal to Marx's influence. Many of the essays in *Semeia* 59 (1992), *Ideological Criticism of Biblical Texts*, ed. David Jobling and Tina Pippin, explore this interpretive terrain. Beginning postmodern interpreters should read the *Semeia* essays in the light of Stephen Fowl's "Texts Don't Have Ideologies" (forthcoming in *Biblical Interpretation*).

The literature on feminist criticism is so expansive that it certainly merits a *What Is . . . ?* volume of its own; readers interested in following this thread of political criticism will do well to consult Janice Capel Anderson's review essay "Mapping Feminist Biblical Criticism: The American Scene, 1983–1990," in *Critical Review of Books in Religion 1991* (Atlanta: Scholars Press, 1991), 21–44. Letty Russell's *Feminist Interpretation of the Bible* (Philadelphia: Westminster Press, 1985), Adela Yarbro Collins's *Feminist Perspectives on Biblical Scholarship* (Atlanta: Scholars Press, 1985), Elisabeth Schüssler Fiorenza's *In Memory of Her* (New York: Crossroad, 1983) and *Bread Not Stone* (Boston: Beacon Press, 1984), and Phyllis Trible's *God and the Rhetoric of Sexuality* and *Texts of Terror* (Philadelphia: Fortress Press, 1978, 1984) are canonical, but these works generally adopt a more or less modern adherence to historical criticism. Readers ought not miss Schüssler Fiorenza's specifically political-critical presidential address to the Society of Biblical Literature, "De-Centering Biblical Interpretation" (*Journal of Biblical Literature* 107 [1985]: 1–17), and her recent *But She Said* (Boston: Beacon Press, 1992), which moves further from her customary historical-critical interests. Carol Newsom provides a provocative reading of Proverbs in "Woman and the Discourse of Patriarchal Wisdom: A Study of Proverbs 1–9," in a collection of feminist studies of the Hebrew Bible, *Gender and Difference in Ancient Israel*, ed. Peggy L. Day (Minneapolis: Fortress Press, 1989), 142–60.

The most postmodern of biblical feminists is Mieke Bal, who deploys a panoply of interpretive devices to analyze the fates of women in biblical narrative. Her demanding but very rewarding—work is best approached via *Lethal Love* (Bloomington: Indiana Univ. Press, 1987).

Most African-American biblical interpreters likewise arrive at their political interpretations by way of historical-critical inquiry. Cain Felder's *Troubling Biblical Waters* (Maryknoll, N.Y.: Orbis, 1989) is an example of a powerful critique of racial bias in biblical interpretation that nonetheless rests on strictly modern warrants; likewise Itumeleng Mosala's Black African–Marxist interpretation in *Biblical Hermeneutics and Black Theology in South Africa* (Grand Rapids, Mich.: Eerdmans, 1989). Several of the essays in *Stony the Road We Trod*, ed. Felder (Minneapolis: Fortress Press, 1991), however, point toward an African-American interpretive stance that does not depend on Eurocentric hermeneutical customs for its legitimation. Michael Cartwright explores these questions via Mikhail Bakhtin's political semiotics and William Henry Gates's studies of African-American "signifyin(g)" in "Ideology and the Interpretation of Scripture in the African-American Christian Tradition" (*Modern Theology* 9 [1993]: 141–58).

Westminster/John Knox Press publishes a noteworthy series of books called Literary Currents in Biblical Interpretation; the series includes numerous volumes that bring an explicit ideological-critical perspective on their readings. Hebrew Bible critics David Gunn, Danna Nolan Fewell, Ilona Rashkow, and David Penchansky, and New Testament critics Elizabeth Castelli and Tina Pippin undertake interpretations informed by Foucault and Jameson (among others). The volume entitled *Reading Between Texts* (Louisville, Ky.: Westminster/John Knox, 1992), edited by Danna Nolan Fewell, includes a useful essay on ideological criticism by Timothy K. Beal, "Ideology and Intertextuality: Surplus of Meaning and Controlling the Means of Production."

The critique of the sacrificial economy that I develop in the closing pages of the chapter comes by way of Luce Irigaray's postmodern feminist criticism; see her "Equal to Whom?" (*differences* 1 [1989]: 59–76), "The Crucified One," in *The Marine Lover of Friedrich Nietzsche* (New York: Columbia Univ. Press, 1991), 164–90, and various essays in *Sexes and Genealogies* (New York: Columbia Univ. Press, 1993). Irigaray's combination of psychoanalytic, political, theological, philosophical, and literary interests can make her work difficult to read, but well worth the effort.

4
Crossing Up the Discourses

While deconstructive interpretation follows readily from post-modern antifoundationalism, and political criticism from postmodern demystifying, there remain other sorts of interpretation that follow more the postmodern resistance to totalities. Chapter 1 suggested that postmodern detotalizing left us in a world with no *pure* discourses; readers who take their cue from this point defy the very notion of discursive purity. These transgressive interpretive practices disregard the modern disciplinary rules and hermeneutical conventions to draw on resources that lie outside the boundaries of modern disciplined scholarship; like venturesome ice cream manufacturers, they cross one discipline's flavor with another's to find out what the result will taste like. These interpreters aim not so much to illuminate the text as to strike a strange fire from the familiar lines of the Bible.

In a sense, then, transgressive interpretations are the positive face of deconstruction: while deconstruction chastens our efforts to ascertain anything about a text, transgressive readers assert audacious "versions" of texts: *in*versions, *extra*versions, *con*versions, *per*versions, *contra*versions, *di*versions, *trans*versions, *sub*versions. Conventional interpretations assume that there is one and only one appropriate context against which to read a text (that is, the historical moment of the text's origin, along with the originator's immediate history). Postmodern readers recognize that this assumption is grounded only in the etiquette that literary interpretation has developed—not in the nature of understanding, or in immutable natural laws of interpretation. They deliberately flout the discursive rules that have separated various theoretical domains in order to produce disruptive interpretive effects. While biblical interpretation customarily sticks within the boundaries of historical (and, to a certain extent, theological) discourse, postmodern interpreters feel free to blur—and cross over ("transgress")—the borderlines that separate biblical interpretation from the literary criticism of fiction, from art history, from psychoanalytic discourses, and so on. When interpreters obey the injunctions of the disciplines whose borders they are crossing, we may describe this dimension of postmodern biblical criticism as "interdisciplinary"; when they mix discourses and genres without careful attention to the rules of the realms they invade, their interpretation is called not so much interdisciplinary as "undisciplined."

This potpourri approach to interpretation amplifies the insight derived from structuralism, that socially constituted discourses are always the result of a "*bricolage*," an improvisatory compilation that constructs its objects (be they shelters, texts, melodies, stews, or whatever) from the various materials at hand. Once again, the discourses whose borders we cross are not themselves pure or homogeneous; even the critics who abide within a single discourse do not all agree on the character or implications of their work. The interpretive *bricoleur* may simply appropriate what she likes from the discourses at hand and fashion from them a context from which generates the interpretive -version that suits her interests.

At this point, we do well to remember that the disciplinary boundaries that seem "natural" to academic life are not defined by natural law or by some Platonic ideal toward which we are evolving. On the contrary, we define disciplines much more by such pragmatic considerations as whether there are numerous scholars investigating a particular set of questions, or whether enough students are likely to enroll in courses. English universities did not teach courses in English literature until the nineteenth century; the sciences were long associated under the disciplinary identity of "natural philosophy." A number of prominent scholars have recently accepted chairs in "humanities" or "liberal arts" as signs that their competence is not circumscribed by disciplinary boundaries; scientists may envision the possibility that various aspects of physics and mathematics, or sociology and psychology and biology, may unite and recombine into emergent new disciplines, while other disciplines (perhaps including religious studies?) may wither away.

Just as academic conventions sustain the illusion that there are self-subsisting identities called "the disciplines," so critical conventions sustain the illusion that there are separable genres of writing that must be interpreted according to their generic qualities. Modern biblical interpreters diligently seek the appropriate genre for interpreting the Gospels, or they specify the particular varieties of psalm genres, for these generic characteristics form a part of the singularly appropriate context for interpreting the Gospels (or Psalms). But these genres exist only as abstract types; interpreters illustrate the shortcomings of genre criticism when no more than a handful of critics can agree on which of the Hellenistic literary genres fits Mark, or which epistolary type suits Romans. Just as there are no pure discourses, no pure disciplines, there are no pure genres—a situation that postmodern readers can exploit to construct their fascinating, surprising interpretations.

For example, some readers call attention to the formal continuity of fictional and nonfictional narrative. The formal character of narrative provides no way to distinguish a narrative that describes events that actually happened from one that reports fictional events; we can only judge narrative sentences true or false based on the claims they seem to be making. One can, of course, quickly judge that some narratives are too improbable to be believed (as, for instance, the claim, "I sprouted wings and flew to work today"), or that one already knows that the facts of a particular matter were different from what a narrative reports (as the claim, "Elvis Presley is alive"). Of course, each of these claims might be true in some unusual sense; I might be describing my morning airplane trip poetically, or I might be claiming that as long as stereos blare "Warden threw a party in the county jail," the spirit of Elvis will live among us. The difficulty in distinguishing "truth" or "history" from "fiction" becomes even greater when a narrative reports events that may be believable, and that we do not already know to be false. Because we lack any way to mark the difference between truthful and fictitious narratives, some interpreters refer to all narrative discourse as "fictive," or fiction-like (although not necessarily "fictional").

One gesture common in New Historicist writing involves beginning an essay with a short account of some incident that seems quite at odds with the "main topic" of the article. Some of these epigraphs come from material contemporary with the matter that the article studies; some come from strikingly different contexts; some purport to be contemporaneous with the subject of the article, but are fictional snippets composed for the sole purpose of complementing the article's thesis. The New Historicist scholars justify this tactic by pointing out that (as we have seen) there is no privileged distinction between "history" and "fiction." If an anecdote about a (fictional) event makes a literary analysis more illuminating, more convincing, then a New Historicist may feel free to employ it as evidence, regardless of whether it is a "factual" account.

If for a moment we suspend the binary opposition "truth/fiction"—if, that is, we agree that the distinction doesn't make a difference—we can

63

cross the Bible's fictive discourse with some other fictive material. We might, for example, read the story of Noah's Ark from a woodworm's point of view (as Julian Barnes does in his *History of the World in 10½ Chapters*), or fill in some of Jesus' many deeds that did not fit into John's Gospel. We would be exploring the postmodern reaches of *intertextuality*, the principle that every text is constituted by other texts; every text borrows words and ideas from predecessor texts, and loans them to successors. When we follow the tracks of these borrowings and lendings, we need not posit an author's conscious allusion. We may instead simply follow a trail of coincident word choices—indeed, perhaps not even the same word, but its punned clone or a foreign-language cognate—through a chain of intertexts to see where the trail leads us. We would not then dismiss such intertextual cross-readings as "untrue" or "unhistorical," but would evaluate them as works of hermeneutical virtuosity: Are they well executed? Are they convincing, or satisfying, or amusing, or instructive? The criteria that we customarily deploy when we judge biblical interpretation depend to a great extent on the cogency of the "true history/erroneous history" dichotomy. We stand to learn much from the criteria we resort to when judging biblical interpretations apart from the "truth/fiction" opposition.

The resources for transgressive readings are limited only by the interpreter's imagination. One may cross over into children's Bibles, or artists' interpretations, or fictional representations of biblical stories, or typography, or media theory (oral/handwritten/block printed/typeset/video/electronic). One's readings may take the shape of familiar interpretive essays, or of parallel but separate interpretive texts, or of performances in the lively, or plastic, or graphic arts.

There is therefore no need to limit our transgressions to the history/fiction distinction; we may likewise dissolve the genre distinction between biblical narratives and the dream reports that form a basis of analytic psychological interpretation. The visionary texts from biblical apocalyptic and biblical parables are only the most obvious candidates for this -version of analytical interpretation ("Well, the bushel basket seems to be your Shadow, and the woman inside it would be the Great Mother"); even the modern readers do as much. A postmodern critic would press further and explore the psychoanalytical significance of the details in any biblical text, on the theory that it is precisely in the selection of details worth retelling that we discern the psychological significance of a text. The details are overdetermined (determined, that is, not by the simple need for a particular word or detail in the narrative, but also by an unconscious significance

64

which that word or detail expresses). We may read the coy exchange between Jesus and the Samaritan Woman as a therapeutic dialogue, or psychoanalyze David's compulsion to obtain beautiful women (Michal, Abigail, Bathsheba) at the cost of death (the Philistines, Nabal, and Uriah, respectively). We may read the biblical texts as the record of a theological unconscious, as of God's Spirit dropping oblique hints to the divine psyche (or at least, of writers' overdetermined expressions of the God who lurks beyond their writings).

Responsible border crossers follow the laws of the country into which they have entered, so they will work hard to make their interpretations acceptable to the inhabitants of each discursive world they visit; they will study their analytic psychology or their psychoanalytic theory diligently, so that their incursions into this alien discourse meet with the approval of local officials. Other border crossers may reason that they are no more bound to local laws than to the laws that bind biblical interpreters to historical inquiries; they will pay less regard to the authority of Freud or Marx and more to the effects one can bring about with an unauthorized version of their theories. These wanton transgressors need observe no criteria other than the exhilarating thrill of an interpretive tour de force.

Some readers elude the customs that regulate interdisciplinary discourse by weaving together texts native to distinct disciplines. These interpreters take the page layout of the Talmud as one cue for their own format. The Talmud is traditionally published with the Mishnah in one column, the Gemara (which comments upon the Mishnah, but also digresses onto other topics) in columns surrounding the Mishnah, and commentaries on both the Mishnah and Gemara at the bottom, or the top. One might learn the same typographical lesson from the *Glossa Ordinaria*, the compilation of Christian medieval biblical interpretation. An edition of the *Glossa Ordinaria* might include an interlinear translation of the biblical text, and a marginal translation; a given edition might also include commentary by one or more scholars as well. (Modern Bibles like the *New Oxford Annotated Bible* give a pale reflection of this robust typographical tradition; the *NOAB* provides the biblical text in the center of the page, with glosses at the lower right corner of the main text block, and commentary at the bottom of the page.) This typographical device generates a textual polyphony; the juxtaposed texts comment on one another, illuminate one another. It breaks down the sense that a single authoritative presence stands behind the monophonic textual voice. Jacques Derrida adopts varieties of this device to great effect in *Glas*, in "Living On/Borderlines," and again in the "Circumfessions" to his collaborative work with Geoff Bennington; he brings about the textual analogue of polyphonic music, or a coffee shop whose various customers all eavesdrop and comment on one another's conversations.

Interpreters who use interpretive devices like these from years past are not necessarily nostalgic for a "good old days" of precritical interpretation; these practices are simply a chronological "impurity" comparable to the methodological impurities that we have surveyed earlier in the chapter. They appear nostalgic only if one regards them from the chronologically determined perspective of modernity, wherein only the most recent methods or movements are legitimate. From a *post*modern perspective, it seems quite odd to suggest that chronological transgressions are taboo, while any sort of disciplinary or generic border crossing may be permitted. The premodern interpretive modes of allegory and midrash reflect several characteristically postmodern interests. One need not be a disciplined expert to see an allegorical relation between the features of a parable and various elements of a given theological (or political, or social) situation; indeed, most nonacademic interpreters resort freely to midrashic amplification or allegorization to make sense of perplexing texts. Allegory and midrash derive their legitimation not from scientific warrants like "What can I prove about this passage's historical context?" but from narrative warrants such as, "Does this explanation fit into the story? Is it a plausible extension of the narrative elements that already constitute the story?"

A cursory scan of postmodern theoretical essays reveals that many critics have found the interpretive modes of allegory and midrash a productive starting point for their textual explorations. Fredric Jameson, for example, has invoked the fourfold system of medieval allegorical interpretation as a basis for his Marxist interpretation of contemporary literature. Medieval interpreters distinguished four dimensions of signification for the biblical text. The literal sense meant the plain, grammatical, historical signification of a passage. The allegorical sense indicated the correspondence between the circumstances of the given passage with other biblical (or sometimes nonbiblical) narratives. The third sense, the tropological, communicated the passage's value for moral instruction. The fourth sense was called the anagogical sense; it connected the passage with the anticipated circumstances of heaven and the end times (as a sort of predictive allegory). For example, the literal reference of the name "Jerusalem" is the city on Zion; its allegorical significance is the Christian church (the city of God's people); the tropological sense is the believer's soul (the dwelling place of the faithful); and the anagogical significance is the heav-

enly city promised in the apocalyptic visions. Jameson appreciates this
system's capacity continually to generate new interpretations, but he suggests that the fourfold approach can be applied more generally if we consider it outside the specifically Christian context from which it emerged.
The literal level remains the same; it concerns the actual events of history,
or the narrated events of the story. Jameson broadens the emphasis of the
allegorical level from a typological relation of biblical texts to the system-
atic correlation of one text to any interpretive context (so one might use
Jamesonian allegory to connect *The Wizard of Oz* to a contemporary political situation). Jameson turns the tropological level from its emphasis
on moral behavior to an emphasis on personal identity; it is the psychological level (Dorothy as ego; the Wizard as superego; the Wicked Witch of
the West, with her winged monkeys, as a threatening id). Finally, Jameson
redefines the anagogical level as the political meaning of the text. While
there are certain difficulties with Jameson's particular scheme, his example suggests that there may be continuing value in this "nostalgic" interpretive approach.

Numerous other postmodern critics have compared their interpretive
ruminations to rabbinic midrash, a mode of interpretation that engages
the (literary) imagination more than the theoretical faculties. Some postmodern interpreters have been deeply impressed with the freedom that
midrash seems to hold out for interpretation; they see Christian allegor-
ism as tediously didactic (concerned as it sometimes was with deriving
dogma from narrative), but rabbinic midrash as almost mischievously
playful. The contrast is overstated; some allegorical interpretation is quite
fantastic, and halakhic midrash is not necessarily lively or venturesome.
One need not, then, indulge in a useless binary opposition between the
specific interpretive practices by which Jews and Christians interwove the
texts of their daily lives with the stories in Scripture. Both midrash and
allegory constitute modes of exposition which part from legitimate modern interpretation in the interest of sustaining and enriching readers' engagement with their texts.

Because allegory and midrash deliberately intercross texts with one another, they constitute a fruitful model for other varieties of postmodern
biblical criticism. They perpetuate a people's engagement with a particular text by connecting the text with the people's lives and concerns—
often despite the absence of any obvious relation between the two. Midrash and allegory permit interpreters to say what they imagine a particular
text might say, had it addressed a particular question. The resulting interpretations, then, are judged not by whether historians agree that the

67

"original" author(s) would have assented to the midrashic interpretation, but by whether the midrash satisfies its audience.

Of course, allegorical interpretation always inspires in some the fear that unauthorized interpreters will make the text say anything they want, that it will become—in Luther's delightful metaphor—a wax nose with no integrity of its own, which willful readers can reshape as they desire. In other words, if we permit transgressive interpretations, we run the risk of abolishing hermeneutical borderlines altogether. This fear—which we have encountered several times earlier—once again fails to reckon with the fact that, although borderlines may be arbitrary, location is not. One may find a place that does not clearly belong to one political (or discursive) district or another, but that does not mean that one is nowhere. Interpreters cannot "make the Bible mean whatever they want it to mean" unless there are audiences that find those interpretations convincing. And thereby hangs the hermeneutical dilemma: No interpretation is self-authenticating, but the validity of any interpretation depends on the assent of some audience. While modern interpreters obey the modern commandment to seek the approval of academically trained disciplinary specialists, postmodern interpreters may seek out a different audience, one that has ears to hear and understand their readings.

The outstanding example of *bricol*-ated, transgressive biblical interpretation is Stephen Moore's extraordinary *Mark and Luke in Poststructuralist Perspective*, a book whose range and verve belie its rather staid title. Moore reads these two Gospels through the intertextual mediation of the works of Jacques Derrida, Jacques Lacan, and James ("Jacques," in French) Joyce. Moore uses puns, coincidences, allusions, and his thorough acquaintance with postmodern theory and the biblical scholarship on Mark and Luke to weave an astonishing interpretive tapestry. While the book is frequently quite difficult to read, its unique combination of ingredients demonstrates the interpretive power of Moore's transgressive imagination.

Although Moore is an erudite navigator of biblical, Derridean, Lacanian, and Joycean criticism, he is not authorized as a citizen of the three last-mentioned academic regions. No one will consult Moore to resolve a psychoanalytic problem; philosophers and literary theoreticians probably will not rush to Moore when they're baffled by Derrida; and Joyce critics will not check *Mark and Luke in Poststructuralist Perspective* for help with *Finnegan's Wake*. Yet by weaving an intertextual network among these narratives and theories, Moore constructs a discourse where his interpretive interests are at home. We judge the extent to which his work is convincing not on the basis of whether it reproduces the interpretive gymnastics that conventional biblical criticism (or criticism of Joyce, Lacan, or Derrida) expects, but on the basis of Moore's having assembled a fascinating textual and theoretical construction.

Few biblical readers are adequately prepared to be imitators of Moore, but virtually all such readers are equipped to undertake their own sorts of transgressive readings. The countless gifts that readers bring to biblical interpretation from various other spheres—domestic life, artistic expression, political activity—provide the materials from which they can *bricolate* their own transgressive readings. These readings will usually not resemble classroom exegetical or homiletical exercises, but (once again) that is not their point.

The point is perhaps best expressed in John Hollander's poem, "The Widener Burying-Ground" (an allusion to Harvard's library). The poem begins by claiming, "In spite of all the learned have said / We hear the voices of the dead." When we interpret texts, we seek the voices of dead authors; but those voices come, not from spectral larynxes, but from our own interpretive efforts:

> Our marginalia all insist
> —Beating the page as with a fist
> Against a silent headstone—that
> The dead whom we are shouting at,
> Though silent to us now, have spoken
> Through us, their stony stillness broken
> By our outcry (*We are the dead*
> *Resounding voices in our stead*).

When we interpret texts, we are the dead (authors). We need not, however, be servile repeaters of silent masters' words; the living will, which brings life to our interpretation, is not constrained by dead intentions. The text does not speak to us—we lend it whatever voice we will. "We strike from silent lines a fire." The fire we strike may be a familiar domestic candle or hearth fire, but we may also light a strange fire to illuminate unfamiliar visions and cast eerie shadows (and perhaps even burn down some dessicated façades).

Those who light strange fires, who undertake unauthorized border crossings, always face risks. There can be no method to ensure that a given performance will succeed, because there will be no authorities to back up the performer. At the same time, the very notion of "success" or "legitimacy," to which transgressive readings appeal, must be different from familiar definitions. Just as performance art can define "success" by so odd a criterion as whether the piece annoys or alienates its audience, so hermeneutical border crossers may set idiosyncratic criteria for their various enterprises (or, just as likely, they may repudiate the idea that there has to be a criterion of success at all). When one repudiates the constraints that academic disciplines and scholarly methods impose, one also forgoes the safety they offer.

Thus, a would-be transgressor who may reject the theoretical underpinnings of conventional biblical criticism may also opt to play the game of interpretation cautiously. A culinary and ceramic interpretation of Paul's dietary advice in Romans might receive a poor grade (or provoke an unfavorable tenure review); a music and video performance of the Annunciation to Mary might alienate one's closest friends. This particular manifestation of postmodern biblical criticism is inextricably bound up with political concerns as well as theoretical arguments about the nature of "criteria" and "disciplines," linking transgressive interpretation with political criticism and deconstruction in an eccentric family of hermeneutical postmodernism.

Further Reading

There are relatively few published examples of the sort of transgressive biblical interpretation I describe here; or, more to the point, there are relatively few examples of self-consciously postmodern academic interpretation (because virtually any nonacademic mode of biblical interpretation transgresses the rules of academic interpretation in one or more ways). The key reference point here is, of course, Stephen Moore's *Mark and Luke in Poststructuralist Perspective* (New Haven: Yale Univ. Press, 1991). Fredric Jameson discusses allegorical interpretation in *The Political Unconscious* (Ithaca, N.Y.: Cornell Univ. Press, 1981). Two of Jacques Derrida's exemplary transgressive exercises are "Living On/Border Lines," trans. James Holbert, in *Deconstruction and Criticism,* Harold Bloom et al. (New York: Seabury Press, 1979), and *Glas,* trans. John P. Leavey, Jr., and Richard Rand (Lincoln: Univ. of Nebraska Press, 1986). One may see subtle border crossers at work in Frederick C. Bauerschmidt's "The Wounds of Christ" (*Journal of Literature & Theology* 5 [1991]: 83–100), Kirk Hughes's "Framing Judas" (a performance work that has been transcribed for publication in *Semeia* 54 [1991]: 223–38), and Timothy K. Beal and Tod Linafelt's "Sifting for Cinders: Strange Fires in Leviticus 10:1–5," forthcoming in *Semeia.* Janice Capel Anderson's

"Feminist Criticism: The Dancing Daughter," her contribution to *Mark and Method* (which she edited with Stephen Moore; Minneapolis: Fortress Press, 1992) exemplifies a specifically feminist approach, which shares much with Bal's and Irigaray's interdisciplinary interpretations. Some of John Dominic Crossan's work, such as *Cliffs of Fall* (New York: Seabury, 1980) and *Raid on the Articulate* (New York: Harper & Row, 1976), also fits under this heading. One might regard Thomas Boomershine's "video translation" of the story of the Gerasene Demoniac, "Out of the Tombs" (American Bible Society, 1991), as a transgression of the academy's "rules of media."

John Hollander's poem appears as the epigraph to his book *The Figure of Echo* (Berkeley: Univ. of California Press, 1981). The story of Noah's woodworm comes from Julian Barnes's book *A History of the World in 10½ Chapters* (New York: Vintage International, 1990).

Although the Ancients cannot have been postmodern in a chronological sense of the term, they were at least nonmodern, and venturesome transgressors could learn a few lessons from their forebears when they begin their ventures in hermeneutical piracy. The visual and plastic art, the glosses and midrashim, translations, mystery plays and passion plays that fail to meet modern interpreters' standards can at least suggest to postmodern critics what it might be like to develop versions of biblical passages without a modern interpretive conscience.

Prelude:
Interpretation as a Kind of
Wri(gh)ting

Richard Rorty has described (and oversimplified) Jacques Derrida's theoretical work as treating "philosophy as a kind of writing." This slogan points toward an important truth about all postmodern discourse: Our interpretations are not authoritative sentences that close the book on interpretive questions but are ventures in persuasion, in seduction. Our interpretations—whether recorded verbally, performed carnally, designed iconically—are wrought from the biblical text, from our audience's hopes and interests and fears, and from the vales of our own imaginations. A postmodern biblical critic constructs an interpretation as something made (just as a cartwright constructs vehicles, or a wheelwright makes wheels). Postmodern biblical criticism is a kind of "wri(gh)ting."

When readers begin to shed their modern habits and change into postmodern vestments, they may feel desperately uncertain. There are few or no rules that might assure them they are doing it right. They may gleefully propound unfettered interpretations but feel betrayed if their colleagues, teachers, or congregations deplore their readings; after all, are they not free to knock down walls, displace and reverse, and pun their ways through reading? Both these hypothetical situations reflect the difference between clear, modern criteria, and ambiguous, elusive postmodern criteria. For the umpteenth time, I repeat: The fact that there are no necessary criteria does not imply that there are no criteria. Even transgressors depend on prior definitions of rules and practices, if only to flout them the more extravagantly.

This is not the place for a recipe by which beginning students might cook up guaranteed foolproof legitimate postmodern interpretations. The existence of such a recipe would falsify many of the themes of the book itself. By what standard could one legitimate the recipe? Is the recipe itself postmodern, or does a clearly defined technical device—the recipe—produce postmodern results through some theoretical alchemy? The "recipe" approach simply does not work here.

On the other hand, would-be postmodernists are not entirely bereft of edifying examples. The "Further Reading" sections of the preceding chapters have supplied numerous sources to which interested students might turn for greater insight into postmodern hermeneutical practices. The works cited there offer both helpful instruction and useful models of characteristically postmodern interpretive maneuvers.

If, as I suggested in the opening remarks, the greatest obstacle to understanding postmodern theory and practice lies in unfamiliarity, readers can most readily elude that obstacle by getting thoroughly acquainted with postmodern critical works. Readers who consult Derrida, Irigaray, Foucault, Kristeva, Lyotard, Jameson, deMan, et al. regularly will acclimate themselves to these critics' theoretical claims, and will learn their customary gestures and expressions. Such readers will then be in the best position to practice postmodern criticism.

Perhaps the greatest preparation for undertaking this different path to biblical interpretation comes when readers begin to practice "thinking the opposite," considering critical possibilities that common wisdom proscribes or conceals. If biblical scholarship stresses its disciplinary autonomy, resistant readers draw on what they have learned in other academic disciplines and, especially, outside "disciplined" learning altogether. Accredited scholars, after all, gain their social recognition by having spent long years acclimating themselves to academic practices; readers who have served apprenticeships in different domains need not discard their experience as irrelevant to biblical interpretation, but can engage problems in interpretation on their own terms. What have they learned about the Pentateuch from their work in soup kitchens and shelters for battered women? How does familiarity with gardening and landscape design prepare readers to interpret apocalyptic literature? Conventional scholarship would allow these elements into the discourse of biblical studies only to the extent that they clarify questions that institutionalized forms of inquiry have already posed (perhaps suggesting that Daniel's visions show the influence of Babylon's famous gardens). A determinedly postmodern interpreter, however, need not concede the sole legitimacy of the questions that modern scholarship authorizes; there are surely interpretive questions apparent to landscapers that have not occurred to historical scholars. Postmodern biblical criticism engages the reader and the Bible not on the terms that any privileged institution (the academy, the synagogue, the church, or the state) sets, but on the terms that interest particular readers and their audiences.

Readers can also "think the opposite" by resisting biblical and interpretive tendencies to pose mutually exclusive interpretive options. Much biblical rhetoric poses either/or alternatives; biblical scholars tend to address problems as though they already know the range of possible alternative solutions. Yet neither case can sustain much interpretive weight. If the Bible deals frequently in "either/or" binary oppositions, these belie the persistent biblical theme that God's ways involve the Derridean tactics of reversal, paradox, and subtle nuance. When scholars decide that there is a problem regarding the Pentateuch's sources, they try to solve that problem by distilling the extant text into its component parts. They forget too easily that the phenomena they notice (narrative repetition, formulaic expressions, idiosyncratic vocabulary) are evidence of intermingled independent sources only once one has adopted a prior set of assumptions. These assumptions decree that such phenomena are uncharacteristic of single-author works, and that such categories as "author," "editor" (or "redactor"), and "independent source" are easily transferable from the situation of modern compositional practices to the situations in which the biblical texts were composed. Once again, such binary oppositions as "single author vs. multiple source" may be misleading. Readers can learn to think about the Pentateuch or the Synoptic Gospels without accepting the initial assumptions that impel modern scholarship to define interpretive options in familiar ways.

Another way of "thinking the opposite" involves the media of biblical interpretation. Whereas interpretive convention dictates that interpretations be delivered in the form of a written essay, postmodern readers can explore infinite other possible media for communicating their interpretations of the Bible. Electronic visual media (videotape, computer video) present the most obvious contemporary examples, but these are only first steps toward interpretive practices that are limited only by interpreters' capacity to think otherwise (and audiences' capacities to receive unfamiliar sorts of biblical interpretation). Live performance (theater, film, oratory) and the plastic and graphic arts (sculpture, painting, drawing) are media in which biblical interpretation has flourished without official biblical scholars' attention or approval; this does not diminish their status as interpretation, but underlines conventional scholarship's narrow interests. The range of interpretive media extends beyond even these, however, to include the practice of biblical interpretation in everyday life (feeding the hungry, giving to those who ask), a venue of interpretation that returns our attention to the political dimensions of postmodern criticism.

Beginning students ought not take any of the foregoing material as a normative prescription for "how to do postmodern criticism," but only as a series of remarks about directions they might adopt. A postmodern primer can only point out to students that the doors they assume to be locked may open easily, if only the students try them. It cannot tell where to go without forfeiting its role as provocateur (rather than as pedagogue; postmodern critics cannot afford to play Polonius). Read works from the suggestions I have provided here; familiarize yourself with the rhythms, the moves, the gestures of the transgressors who have preceded you. Then venture out on your own.

This all may seem more daunting, more laborious than the exhilarating freedom that postmodern criticism seemed to promise. Such an austere impression recognizes that postmodern thinking banishes landmarks and guarantees exactly as much as it dissolves the constraints and assumptions that hinder readers. No one can manage without some of these land-marks. This book, for instance, remains within the bounds of conventional English syntax, eschews even the familiar typographical complications of footnotes and endnotes, and respects the customs of academic discourse. The same landmarks that orient us, however, always divert us from other paths, so that the book's simple syntax, its monophonic typography and academic courtesy have obscured some points of postmodern thought, which one cannot communicate via strictly conventional prose.

Of course, we cannot avoid the problems of responsibility either by simply repeating the steps our interpretive Fathers taught us, or by worrying ourselves to death over precisely how to deviate from their patterns. As Jean-François Lyotard reminds us:

> The post-modern artist or writer is in the position of a philosopher: the text he [sic] writes or the work he creates is not in principle governed by preestablished rules and cannot be judged according to the dominant judgment, by the application of given categories to this text or work. Such rules and categories are what the work or text is investigating. (*The Postmodern Explained* [Minneapolis: Univ. of Minnesota Press, 1993], 15)

The rules for postmodern interpretations become manifest only after the fact; we will not know how to judge such interpretations until after we have wrought them. The thing to do is just to go ahead, to bricolate the

-versions that seem right from the materials we find at hand and to present our interpretations to our audiences, the readers and hearers to whom
we are accountable. Propound your own -versions of the age-old stories;
spin unfamiliar text-iles from the familiar threads we have been given;
steal away across the border to smuggle an unauthorized insight into a
hermeneutical Babylon; "strike from silent lines a fire"; wri(gh)t the interpretations that modern biblical hermeneutics has forbidden.

Index